The
PISCES
Path

YOUR DAILY 2026 HOROSCOPE GUIDE

AMANDA M CLARKE

Copyright © Amanda M Clarke 2026
KORU Publishing

All rights reserved. All content, materials, and intellectual property in this book or any other platform owned by Koru Publishing are protected by copyright laws. This includes text, images, graphics, videos, audio, software, and any other form of content that may be produced by Koru Publishing.

No part of this content may be reproduced, distributed, or transmitted in any form or by any means without the prior written permission of Koru Publishing. This means that you cannot copy, reproduce, or use any of the content in this book for commercial or personal purposes without the express written consent of Koru Publishing.

Unauthorized use of any copyrighted material owned by Koru Publishing may result in legal action being taken against you. Koru Publishing reserves the right to pursue all available legal remedies against any individual or entity found to be infringing on its copyright.

In summary, Koru Publishing © 2024 holds exclusive rights to all the content produced by it, and any unauthorized use of such content will result in legal action.

KORU Publishing

KORU (Maori;NZ)
A symbol of spiritual growth and spiritual connection.

Rocky Point Townhouse, CHRISTMAS ISLAND, Western Australia 6798

ISBN: 978-1-923614-04-8

More on the Bookshelves at www.theliteraryoracle.com

Disclaimer: The Pisces Path: Your daily 2026 horoscope guide book provides information on astrological readings and intuative interpretations, it is not intended as a substitute for professional advice, diagnosis, or treatment. The information contained in this book is provided for educational and entertainment purposes only and is not meant to be taken as specific advice for individual circumstances. The author and publisher make no representations or warranties with respect to the accuracy or completeness of the contents of this book and specifically disclaim any implied warranties of merchantability or fitness for a particular purpose. The reader should always consult with a licensed professional for any specific concerns or questions. The author and publisher shall not be liable for any loss or damage caused or alleged to have been caused, directly or indirectly, by the information contained in this book. The use of this book is at the reader's sole risk

More from Amanda Clarke
The Literary Oracle
www.theliteracyoracle.com

The "Daily Guidance" series offers an innovative approach to finding spiritual wisdom and practical advice. Each book in the series is a unique tool designed for daily introspection and decision-making. Readers are invited to meditate on a question or seek general guidance for the day, then flip to a random page in the book. The page they land on provides a personalized message from various spiritual sources, such as angels, tarot, or spirit animals. With each turn of the page, these books deliver insightful, positive messages and mantras to inspire personal growth and provide clarity on life's daily challenges and decisions.

Other books in this series:-
The Angelic Oracles
Daily Angel Tarot Reading
Mystic Tarot Cat
Oracle of the Tarot Cat
Vibes Unveiled
Spirit Animal Oracle
Answers from the Oracles
Messages from the Angels

Supporting Indie Authors

Love your daily guidance? You can grab more of my books direct from The Literary Oracle: www.theliteraryoracle.com

Buying direct means:
- Much better prices for you + free shipping.
- More support for me as an indie author
- More magical books in your hands

My books are also available worldwide through online bookstores, but direct purchases help keep the magic flowing.

Thank you for supporting indie creativity!

Scan me

Welcome to The Pisces Path: Your Daily 2026 Horoscope Guide — your intuitive, heart-centered companion for the year ahead. Crafted for the compassionate, imaginative, and quietly wise Pisces, this guide honors the way you move through life — with deep feeling, boundless empathy, and a soul that sees what others often miss.

Inside, you'll find daily horoscopes paired with affirmations designed to flow in harmony with your natural gifts. Each page offers guidance to help you navigate 2026 with grace — whether you're strengthening your relationships, pursuing creative dreams, tending to your well-being, or simply learning to trust the tides of change.

This isn't about rushing forward — it's about surrendering to flow. As you turn each page, you'll receive gentle reminders, encouragement, and cosmic whispers urging you to embrace your intuition and trust your inner wisdom. Let this be the year you listen deeply, love fully, and step into the magic of living in alignment with your heart and the stars.

The Answers You Seek

Are Within

January 2026

Pisces
01 January 2026

Pisces, the year begins with a soft yet powerful lunar influence tugging at your emotional tides. You may feel drawn inward, reflecting on the past year while sensing the quiet whisper of fresh beginnings. Your intuition is sharp today—pay attention to the subtle cues that arrive in dreams or fleeting thoughts. Even in solitude, you're surrounded by support from unseen realms. Don't rush resolutions; instead, allow inspiration to drift naturally toward you, much like the ocean current. Trust that clarity will surface when the timing is right.

Affirmation & Gratitude

I trust my inner compass and welcome the gentle guidance flowing into my life today.

Pisces
02 January 2026

Today, Pisces, your creative waters stir with energy. Venus highlights connections, reminding you that love and inspiration are intertwined. A conversation could spark a new direction, offering insights into how you wish to express yourself. You might feel slightly sensitive to others' moods, so protect your energy without closing off your heart. Journaling or painting could be especially healing. Relationships benefit from honesty and tenderness, even in small gestures. Allow yourself to dream big, but stay anchored in practicality when it comes to commitments.

Affirmation & Gratitude

I open my heart to creativity and let compassion guide my words and actions with others.

Pisces
03 January 2026

Pisces, Mercury lights up your communication sector today, and your words carry weight. Share your ideas but avoid overexplaining—your intuition often speaks louder than logic. A chance message, phone call, or online exchange could reveal an opportunity worth exploring. Be cautious about scattering your focus; instead, choose one project or conversation and give it your full presence. Others admire your perspective, even if you underestimate your wisdom. Your sensitivity is your gift, not a weakness—use it to connect meaningfully.

Affirmation & Gratitude

I speak with clarity and listen with openness, knowing my voice matters in the world today.

Pisces
04 January 2026

Energy shifts today, Pisces, as Mars influences your routines. You may feel the urge to take control of health, work, or daily habits. A small adjustment—like drinking more water or organizing your workspace—can ripple into larger transformation. Don't let overwhelm stop you; start with one thing and let momentum build. You might feel tension if expectations clash with your desire for rest. Balance action with compassion for your own limits. Progress isn't about speed, but about steady intention.

Affirmation & Gratitude

I embrace small changes that build strong foundations for my wellbeing and daily peace of mind.

Pisces
05 January 2026

Pisces, the Moon highlights your emotional depth today, and you may feel waves of nostalgia or yearning for connection. Old memories might surface, nudging you to release lingering attachments. This is not a day to suppress feelings; instead, honor them with gentle reflection. A quiet walk in nature or meditation can help you process and reset. You have the ability to heal yourself by allowing emotions to flow like water, without judgment. Healing starts with self-acceptance.

Affirmation & Gratitude

I honor my emotions as part of my growth, allowing healing and love to flow freely through me.

Pisces
06 January 2026

Today is about vision, Pisces. Jupiter expands your horizons, encouraging you to dream beyond your current circumstances. Consider what goals truly resonate with your heart rather than what you think you "should" pursue. Travel, study, or spiritual exploration may call to you, even in small ways. Watch for synchronicities guiding your next step. Remember, expansion comes not from doing everything at once but by aligning with what feels authentic. Trust the universe to meet you halfway.

Affirmation & Gratitude

I welcome expansion in alignment with my truth, knowing the universe supports my highest vision.

Pisces
07 January 2026

Pisces, your compassionate nature is your strength today, but avoid pouring too much of yourself into others without boundaries. Saturn reminds you of responsibility—your dreams require structure to thrive. Reflect on commitments and ensure they match your true desires. A project may demand patience, but the rewards will be lasting if you invest steadily. Balance generosity with self-respect. You can be both kind and firm, both dreamy and grounded. This duality is where your power lies.

Affirmation & Gratitude

I balance kindness with boundaries, nurturing my dreams with patience and discipline.

Pisces
08 January 2026

Pisces, today you may feel the tension between your need for solitude and the demands of others. The cosmos pushes you to find balance rather than extremes. A friend or colleague might lean on you for advice, but remember to keep your energy intact. Empathy doesn't mean overextending yourself. This is a day to test boundaries while still offering your natural warmth. Dreams may be vivid tonight, carrying insights from your subconscious. Write them down—the messages could serve as gentle guidance for the weeks ahead.

Affirmation & Gratitude

I give support with love, while honoring my own need for space and replenishment.

Pisces
09 January 2026

Energy rises, Pisces, as the Moon aligns with action-driven Mars. You may feel motivated to tackle something that's been sitting on your to-do list far too long. This is a wonderful day for clearing clutter, finishing projects, or asserting yourself where you've been hesitant. Trust your instincts but temper impulsive actions—especially around financial or emotional investments. Someone may test your patience, but instead of reacting, use this moment to show how steady you can be under pressure. Progress is steady when directed with focus.

Affirmation & Gratitude

I move forward with courage and clarity, taking action that supports my highest good.

Pisces
10 January 2026

Today the Moon highlights relationships, Pisces, and you might feel more attuned to the needs of those close to you. A loved one could open up, or you may find yourself reflecting on how balanced your partnerships are. Avoid falling into the trap of giving more than you receive—relationships flourish when energy flows both ways. If single, this is an excellent day to notice how your self-worth influences your connections. Open your heart but remain discerning about who earns a place within it.

Affirmation & Gratitude

I welcome relationships built on equality, kindness, and respect, knowing I deserve genuine love.

Pisces
11 January 2026

Pisces, your intuition is strong today as Neptune, your ruling planet, whispers truths just below the surface. Pay close attention to subtle signals—whether a gut feeling, a sign in conversation, or a dream fragment. These are guiding lights meant to steer you toward alignment. You may feel tempted to doubt yourself, but the universe encourages you to trust your inner knowing. Creative inspiration also flows easily now—write, paint, or express yourself in whatever form feels most natural.

Affirmation & Gratitude

I trust my intuition completely, allowing it to guide me with wisdom and clarity.

Pisces
12 January 2026

Practical matters surface today, Pisces, as Saturn calls for responsibility. This isn't about restriction—it's about building the life you dream of on solid ground. Bills, schedules, or work tasks may demand focus. Though it may feel tedious, attending to these details clears the path for your creative flow later. Avoid procrastination, as it only creates stress. Structure is your ally now; once the framework is steady, your imagination has the freedom to soar.

Affirmation & Gratitude

I embrace structure and responsibility, knowing they create freedom for my dreams to thrive.

Pisces
13 January 2026

Pisces, the cosmic weather brings clarity around career or long-term goals. You might feel a sudden realization about where your efforts are truly valued. This could spark motivation to step into a role that feels more aligned with your talents. Don't be afraid to ask yourself tough questions about what success really means to you. Your compassion and creativity are strengths, but they thrive best when supported by direction. Use today to set intentions that resonate with your soul.

Affirmation & Gratitude

I align my ambitions with my heart, creating a life of purpose and fulfillment.

Pisces
14 January 2026

Emotional depth runs high today, Pisces, as the Moon pulls you into inner reflection. Family or home matters may demand attention, or you may simply feel called to nurture yourself more fully. Don't underestimate the healing power of rest, comfort, and familiar spaces. Cooking a meal, listening to music, or speaking with loved ones can ground you. Allow yourself to retreat without guilt. Sometimes the greatest growth comes not from pushing forward, but from restoring your emotional energy.

Affirmation & Gratitude

I find strength in rest and healing, allowing myself to be nurtured and renewed.

Pisces
15 January 2026

Pisces, today invites you to explore new ideas and possibilities. The planetary energy highlights curiosity and learning, making it a wonderful time to study, research, or dive into a subject that has fascinated you. A conversation could open doors or shift how you see something important. Stay open to perspectives outside your comfort zone—they may hold the spark you've been seeking. Even a casual chat or article can deliver a life-changing insight. Trust that knowledge is flowing toward you now.

Affirmation & Gratitude

I welcome new insights with curiosity, knowing that every lesson enriches my path.

Pisces
16 January 2026

Your energy feels pulled between practicality and imagination today, Pisces. While part of you wants to dream and float, the other side is aware of responsibilities waiting. Don't feel pressured to choose—find ways to weave the two together. Use imagination to solve a practical problem, or let a routine task become a meditative ritual. You'll notice that inspiration often comes when you ground it in action. Avoid escaping into distractions; instead, let your creativity uplift even the most ordinary parts of life.

Affirmation & Gratitude

I blend imagination with practicality, creating harmony between dreams and responsibilities.

Pisces
17 January 2026

Relationships come into focus today, Pisces, and the energy encourages deeper conversations. You may feel called to share something from your heart or listen to someone reveal their truth. Avoid avoiding—honesty brings healing now. Even if emotions feel intense, trust that clarity is worth the discomfort. This could be a turning point in understanding how you relate to others. If single, you may recognize a pattern you're ready to release. Allow openness and courage to guide your interactions.

Affirmation & Gratitude

I honor truth and vulnerability, knowing that honesty deepens my connections.

Pisces
18 January 2026

Pisces, today feels like a cosmic reset. The stars encourage you to release clutter—both physical and emotional—that no longer serves your growth. You may feel the urge to clean, rearrange, or simplify. On a deeper level, this is about letting go of outdated beliefs or attachments. Imagine yourself as water, flowing freely and unblocked by old debris. The lighter you travel, the easier it is to embrace new opportunities waiting on the horizon. Today's cleansing is tomorrow's liberation.

Affirmation & Gratitude

I release what no longer serves me, creating space for fresh energy to enter.

Pisces
19 January 2026

Your intuition is exceptionally sharp today, Pisces. Pay attention to dreams, synchronicities, or sudden inner nudges. The universe is whispering answers if you're willing to pause and listen. Don't dismiss what feels "coincidental"—it may be direct guidance. Spend quiet time near water or in meditation to amplify your inner voice. Your sensitivity allows you to detect energies others miss, making you a natural guide. Use this gift not just for others, but also to navigate your own path.

Affirmation & Gratitude

I trust the signs around me and honor my intuition as my compass.

Pisces
20 January 2026

Energy shifts dramatically today, Pisces, as the Sun moves into Aquarius, activating your subconscious zone. This is a period of reflection, inner healing, and preparation before your birthday season begins. You may feel quieter than usual, preferring rest, solitude, or spiritual practices over external demands. Use this time wisely—it's a chance to restore your spirit and prepare intentions for the new solar cycle. Dreams may reveal guidance, so keep a journal nearby. Reflection is the key now.

Affirmation & Gratitude

I embrace stillness and reflection, knowing rest prepares me for powerful new beginnings.

Pisces
21 January 2026

Pisces, the cosmos encourages you to balance your spiritual insights with real-world action today. You may receive a burst of inspiration or clarity about a next step, but don't just let it drift away. Anchor the idea in writing, planning, or taking one practical action. Even the smallest effort can set energy in motion. You'll feel more empowered when your visions are supported by tangible progress. Trust your imagination, but give it wings by grounding it in reality.

Affirmation & Gratitude

I take small steps that transform dreams into reality, aligning vision with action.

Pisces
22 January 2026

Pisces, today highlights friendships and community connections. You may feel called to spend time with like-minded souls or join a group that shares your interests. Collaboration brings both joy and opportunity, so don't isolate yourself when the universe is nudging you to expand. A friend's words may hold unexpected wisdom, reminding you of the power of shared experiences. Be mindful, though—protect your energy if someone tries to lean too heavily on you. Balance giving with receiving. The right tribe uplifts and inspires your path.

Affirmation & Gratitude

I welcome connections that nourish my soul and bring inspiration into my life.

Pisces
23 January 2026

The cosmos urges you to look at your long-term goals today, Pisces. Where do you see yourself in five or ten years? Are your current actions supporting that vision, or are adjustments needed? Don't be afraid to think big, but also break your dreams into manageable steps. A mentor, boss, or colleague may give feedback that feels challenging but ultimately pushes you closer to alignment. This is a day to set intentions around career, legacy, and your place in the world.

Affirmation & Gratitude

I align my daily steps with my greater vision, building a future filled with purpose.

Pisces
24 January 2026

Pisces, your emotional sensitivity is heightened today, and you may feel deeply attuned to the moods of those around you. While this can be draining, it's also a reminder of your unique gift. Use your empathy wisely—don't absorb what isn't yours. Creative outlets like writing, painting, or music can help you process emotions productively. Be gentle with yourself if you feel overwhelmed. Sometimes, retreating for a little solitude is the healthiest way to reset and regain clarity.

Affirmation & Gratitude

I protect my energy and honor my sensitivity as a powerful gift.

Pisces
25 January 2026

Today's energy encourages you to dig into your inner world, Pisces. A spiritual practice—whether meditation, journaling, or quiet contemplation—may reveal truths you've been avoiding. The cosmos is asking you to face a hidden fear or release an old wound. While it might feel uncomfortable, remember that transformation begins with acknowledgement. Trust that healing is within reach. This is also a powerful day for forgiveness, whether toward yourself or someone else. Release opens the door to peace.

Affirmation & Gratitude

I allow healing to flow by releasing the past and welcoming forgiveness into my heart.

Pisces
26 January 2026

Pisces, you may feel a surge of inspiration today that makes you want to leap forward with fresh ideas. While enthusiasm is beautiful, ground your vision before acting impulsively. Write down your plans, create a list, or map out your dreams. Practical steps will help your imagination take form. A conversation with someone supportive could bring validation and encouragement. Trust in your creativity, but remember that patience and structure give your dreams the space to grow strong.

Affirmation & Gratitude

I channel my inspiration into grounded action, turning imagination into lasting creation.

Pisces
27 January 2026

Today may bring unexpected revelations, Pisces, especially in your relationships or daily routines. Something hidden could surface, giving you clarity you didn't know you needed. Instead of resisting, embrace the shift—it's clearing the way for greater authenticity. Pay attention to body signals; your intuition may show up through physical sensations as much as through thoughts. Be open to sudden insight, but don't rush decisions. Let the information settle before you act. Transformation begins with awareness.

Affirmation & Gratitude

I embrace new truths with openness, knowing they guide me toward greater authenticity.

Pisces
28 January 2026

Pisces, today is about balance between rest and productivity. You may feel the urge to withdraw, yet obligations still call. Instead of choosing one over the other, schedule your day so you can honor both. Tackle essential tasks, but also carve out time to recharge your spirit. This balance ensures you don't run dry. A bath, nap, or quiet meditation could work wonders. Remember, your energy is precious; conserving it is part of thriving.

Affirmation & Gratitude

I balance action with rest, honoring my energy as sacred and essential.

Pisces
29 January 2026

Pisces, today you may feel pulled between wanting to focus on your responsibilities and the strong need to retreat into your inner world. The stars highlight balance—neither ignoring duties nor sacrificing your spiritual wellbeing. Practical matters may take priority early in the day, but carve out space later for rest, reflection, or creative play. A conversation could help you realize you've been holding onto too much. Delegate where possible and allow yourself to breathe. Simplicity is your friend now.

Affirmation & Gratitude

I balance responsibility with self-care, honoring both my duties and my spirit.

Pisces
30 January 2026

Energy is vibrant today, Pisces, with the Moon activating your social sector. You may feel more outgoing than usual, enjoying laughter, conversation, or shared experiences. This is an excellent day to reach out to friends, plan a gathering, or connect with someone you've lost touch with. Inspiration often comes through others, so listen closely—someone may share words that shift your perspective. Be mindful not to overcommit, though; joy comes from genuine connection, not spreading yourself too thin.

Affirmation & Gratitude

I celebrate connection and welcome joy through meaningful conversations and laughter with others.

Pisces
31 January 2026

Pisces, today brings reflection on endings and beginnings. The cosmos encourages you to tie up loose ends before entering a fresh cycle. This could mean finishing a project, paying attention to financial details, or even letting go of a habit that's outlived its usefulness. You may feel a bit nostalgic, but trust that closure brings freedom. Tonight, allow yourself a ritual of release—journaling, lighting a candle, or meditation will help you prepare for the next chapter.

Affirmation & Gratitude

I release the old with gratitude, preparing myself for fresh beginnings filled with hope.

February 2026

Pisces
01 February 2026

A new month begins with fresh energy, Pisces, and you may feel a renewed sense of possibility. This is a powerful day to set intentions for the weeks ahead. What do you want to call into your life? Focus on areas of growth, healing, and joy. Avoid scattering your energy—choose two or three intentions and dedicate yourself to them. The universe is listening, so be clear about your desires. Alignment begins with deliberate thought and small, consistent action.

Affirmation & Gratitude

I set clear intentions, trusting the universe to meet me halfway.

Pisces
02 February 2026

Pisces, your sensitivity is heightened today, and you may feel deeply tuned into the emotions of those around you. While this can be a gift, be mindful not to take on burdens that aren't yours. Protect your energy with grounding rituals—walk barefoot, meditate, or spend time near water. This is also a creative day, with ideas flowing more freely than usual. Use your imagination to solve a problem or express yourself through art or words.

Affirmation & Gratitude

I honor my sensitivity as strength and protect my energy with loving boundaries.

Pisces
03 February 2026

The stars highlight finances and stability today, Pisces. You may find yourself reflecting on money management, investments, or long-term security. This is not a day to overspend, but rather to plan wisely. A practical approach now creates peace of mind later. Don't shy away from seeking advice if you need it—clarity around financial matters is empowering. Remember, abundance flows not only from income but also from gratitude and wise stewardship of what you already have.

Affirmation & Gratitude

I manage my resources with wisdom, trusting abundance to flow steadily into my life.

Pisces
04 February 2026

Pisces, today's energy highlights growth and expansion. You may feel called toward travel, study, or exploring new perspectives. Even if you can't physically journey, open your mind through reading, conversation, or exploring a subject that sparks curiosity. Opportunities may appear suddenly, inviting you to step outside your comfort zone. Say yes to growth, but don't overwhelm yourself with too much at once. Trust that the universe will guide you toward what expands your soul.

Affirmation & Gratitude

I welcome expansion and embrace new opportunities with an open and curious heart.

Pisces
05 February 2026

Pisces, today you may feel a pull between what's practical and what your heart longs for. Work, deadlines, or responsibilities could weigh on you, but your spirit craves freedom and expression. The cosmos asks you to find creative ways to blend the two. Perhaps bring imagination into your work or give yourself permission to dream while handling routine tasks. Avoid the temptation to escape through distractions—face matters with presence and compassion. You'll discover flow when you stop fighting against the rhythm of the day.

Affirmation & Gratitude

I flow with life's rhythm, blending responsibility with imagination in every step.

Pisces
06 February 2026

Emotions run deep today, Pisces, and you may feel waves of nostalgia or yearning. The Moon stirs your heart, reminding you of people, places, or dreams that have shaped you. Instead of dwelling, allow yourself to honor these feelings as part of your story. Transformation comes when you use the past as wisdom, not as chains. Healing conversations may arise, especially with family or close friends. Choose honesty over avoidance; vulnerability brings connection.

Affirmation & Gratitude

I honor my past as a teacher while embracing the present as my gift.

Pisces
07 February 2026

Pisces, today highlights relationships and partnerships. The stars encourage you to reflect on whether the give-and-take in your connections feels balanced. If you've been giving more than you receive, it's time to address it gently but firmly. If single, you may recognize what you truly want in a partner—clarity that attracts alignment. Love doesn't need to be complicated; it thrives on honesty and mutual respect. Let today be about strengthening bonds through openness and kindness.

Affirmation & Gratitude

I welcome balanced, loving relationships built on truth and respect.

Pisces
08 February 2026

Pisces, your intuition is like a lighthouse today, guiding you through uncertainty. Pay close attention to gut feelings, dreams, or subtle signs—they're carrying messages from your higher self. Even the smallest nudge may redirect you toward something important. Don't let self-doubt drown out your inner voice. Write down intuitive hits to see how they connect later. Spiritual practices are powerful now—meditation, prayer, or journaling can anchor insights. Trust that the universe is speaking clearly.

Affirmation & Gratitude

I listen to my intuition and trust its wisdom to guide me with clarity.

Pisces
09 February 2026

The cosmic energy highlights creativity and play, Pisces. You may feel inspired to try something new, whether it's painting, dancing, or simply letting yourself have fun. Joy is a powerful healer—don't underestimate it. Children or younger people may inspire you with their openness and spontaneity. If work feels heavy, take short breaks to infuse lightness into your day. Play isn't wasted time; it's fuel for your spirit and a reminder of the beauty of being alive.

Affirmation & Gratitude

I embrace joy and creativity, letting play nourish my spirit.

Pisces
10 February 2026

Pisces, today's energy is grounding, helping you focus on daily routines, health, and wellbeing. Ask yourself: are your habits supporting your body and mind, or draining them? Small steps—like stretching, eating mindfully, or staying hydrated—can have profound effects now. Mars supports action, so it's an ideal day to start a positive routine. Avoid pushing too hard, though; slow and steady wins. Treat your body as a temple, not a machine, and it will reward you with vitality.

Affirmation & Gratitude

I care for my body with love, creating habits that nourish my wellbeing.

Pisces
11 February 2026

A spiritual softness surrounds you today, Pisces. The cosmos opens a window into your inner world, encouraging reflection and gentle self-discovery. This is not a day for rushing or forcing outcomes. Allow space for stillness; wisdom will rise in the quiet moments. Creative writing, art, or simply daydreaming can feel deeply fulfilling. You may receive signs that affirm you're on the right path—trust them. Your sensitivity is a superpower, guiding you toward what resonates with your soul.

Affirmation & Gratitude

I find wisdom in stillness and trust the signs that guide me forward.

Pisces
12 February 2026

Pisces, today the stars encourage you to find balance between work and home. You may feel torn between obligations and the desire for comfort or rest. While it's tempting to focus on only one, try weaving the two together. A tidy space can bring mental clarity, and a brief pause at work can restore energy. Family matters may arise, offering a chance to nurture connections or address something long avoided. Don't shy away—your compassionate nature can heal tension.

Affirmation & Gratitude

I create harmony between my responsibilities and my need for comfort and connection.

Pisces
13 February 2026

Relationships take center stage today, Pisces, and you may notice how much you've grown in what you want from others. Patterns from the past could resurface, but this time you see them with clearer eyes. Instead of repeating cycles, you're ready to choose differently. A partner or close friend may bring an important conversation. Listen, but don't silence your needs. Mutual respect and understanding strengthen bonds. Remember, your voice deserves to be heard just as much as your heart.

Affirmation & Gratitude

I honor my needs and welcome relationships built on mutual respect and truth.

Pisces
14 February 2026

Valentine's Day carries a dreamy energy for you, Pisces. Whether you're partnered or single, the universe encourages you to embrace love in all its forms—not just romance. Self-love is especially highlighted, reminding you to treat yourself with tenderness and care. Acts of kindness ripple outward, so let your compassion shine today. A romantic spark may ignite, or a friend could offer unexpected warmth. Love, in any expression, is your soul's language, and today you're fluent in it.

Affirmation & Gratitude

I give and receive love freely, starting with myself as the source.

Pisces
15 February 2026

Pisces, the cosmos invites you to reflect on your goals and where you've placed your energy. Are you building toward something that truly inspires you, or simply following routine? Today offers clarity, helping you see where adjustments are needed. Don't be afraid to shift course if something no longer aligns. The universe rewards authenticity. Write down your goals and consider whether they still resonate. Even small pivots now can set you on a truer, more fulfilling path.

Affirmation & Gratitude

I align my goals with my soul's truth, trusting the universe to support me.

Pisces
16 February 2026

Today's energy emphasizes communication, Pisces. Conversations may feel more meaningful, carrying truths that can shift how you see a situation. Be open but also discerning—some words inspire, while others may test your boundaries. Express your feelings honestly but gently. You may also receive a message or sign that feels perfectly timed. Writing, journaling, or even recording your thoughts can help you process insights. Don't underestimate the healing power of your words—they can inspire and soothe others.

Affirmation & Gratitude

I speak with honesty and compassion, letting my words carry truth and healing.

Pisces
17 February 2026

Pisces, emotions run high today, but they serve a purpose. You may feel more vulnerable than usual, yet this vulnerability is a gift—it reveals what truly matters. Don't bottle it up; instead, allow safe spaces for release, whether through tears, art, or deep conversation. By honoring your feelings, you clear stagnant energy and make space for renewal. The Moon encourages you to trust your heart, even when logic doesn't have the answers. Healing begins with self-acceptance.

Affirmation & Gratitude

I honor my emotions as sacred, trusting that vulnerability is strength.

Pisces
18 February 2026

The Sun moves into Pisces today, beginning your birthday season and personal new year. This is your cosmic reset, Pisces—a time to celebrate who you are and the journey ahead. Energy feels renewed, and you may feel both reflective and excited. Set intentions for your year, focusing on authenticity, creativity, and spiritual growth. Your sensitivity and wisdom shine now, drawing others toward your light. Don't dim yourself to fit in; this is your time to step forward boldly.

Affirmation & Gratitude

I celebrate my unique light and welcome the new year of my soul with joy.

Pisces
19 February 2026

Pisces, the first full day of your solar season amplifies your energy, reminding you that it's time to embrace your individuality. The stars encourage you to prioritize your own path rather than bending to others' expectations. You may feel a surge of creativity and inspiration, but don't let self-doubt creep in. Your compassionate heart can sometimes make you defer, but today is about stepping into your truth. Own your desires and let your presence be felt—this is your moment to shine.

Affirmation & Gratitude

I honor my authentic self and step confidently into my season of renewal.

Pisces
20 February 2026

The cosmos highlights your finances and resources today, Pisces. This is a good day to review budgets, bills, or spending habits. It's not about restriction but about creating stability that supports your dreams. You may realize that aligning your money with your values brings peace. Avoid impulsive purchases, especially if they're a temporary escape. Instead, focus on long-term goals. Security now provides freedom later. A small adjustment in how you manage resources can ripple into big rewards.

Affirmation & Gratitude

I align my resources with my values, creating stability that supports my dreams.

Pisces
21 February 2026

Pisces, today brings insight into your personal growth and values. You may feel clearer about what truly matters to you, and this clarity helps you say "no" to what drains you. A conversation or reflection may reveal where you've been undervaluing yourself. Don't settle—your worth is not up for negotiation. By honoring your inner truth, you set a higher standard in all areas of life. Growth often comes from releasing what no longer resonates.

Affirmation & Gratitude

I know my worth and align with what truly honors my soul.

Pisces
22 February 2026

The Moon highlights communication today, Pisces, encouraging you to speak your truth. Conversations flow easily, and your words may carry healing for others. Be mindful not to scatter your energy by overexplaining—simple honesty is enough. You may also receive an important message or news that shifts your perspective. Writing or journaling could bring clarity if your mind feels full. This is a day where words become medicine, so use them with care and intention.

Affirmation & Gratitude

I use my words wisely, bringing clarity and healing through honest expression.

Pisces
23 February 2026

Pisces, the stars illuminate your home and inner world today. You may feel drawn to nurture your environment, whether through cleaning, decorating, or simply enjoying comfort at home. Emotional matters connected to family could surface, offering a chance for healing. Don't shy away from heartfelt conversations—they can strengthen bonds. If you've been feeling restless, grounding yourself in your space can restore peace. The more secure you feel within, the more easily you thrive outside.

Affirmation & Gratitude

I create peace within my home and heart, knowing both nurture my soul.

Pisces
24 February 2026

The energy today is expansive, Pisces, urging you to look beyond your current perspective. You may feel inspired to learn, travel, or explore new spiritual practices. Even a small shift—like trying a new book, class, or conversation—can open doors. Trust that curiosity leads to growth. Opportunities may come through unexpected sources, so keep your mind and heart open. This is a day for broadening horizons and remembering there's more available than what you see right now.

Affirmation & Gratitude

I expand my mind and spirit, welcoming opportunities that bring growth.

Pisces
25 February 2026

Pisces, today's energy encourages reflection and inner healing. You may feel quieter than usual, drawn to solitude or spiritual practices. This is not withdrawal—it's restoration. The cosmos invites you to tend to your soul, perhaps by meditating, journaling, or simply resting. If you've been carrying burdens, today offers a chance to lay them down. Pay attention to dreams or signs; the universe is speaking softly but clearly. Allow stillness to renew your strength and clarity.

Affirmation & Gratitude

I embrace quiet moments, knowing stillness restores my spirit and guides me forward.

Pisces
26 February 2026

Pisces, today's cosmic energy encourages you to reconnect with your creative spirit. The stars highlight your natural talents, and you may feel inspired to paint, write, sing, or simply daydream. Don't dismiss these impulses—they're channels for your soul's voice. Someone may compliment your gifts, reminding you how impactful they are, even if you underestimate yourself. Avoid perfectionism; creativity is about expression, not judgment. Let joy be your guide, and remember that play often unlocks your deepest inspiration.

Affirmation & Gratitude

I allow creativity to flow freely, expressing my soul without judgment.

Pisces
27 February 2026

The focus shifts to your health and wellbeing today, Pisces. You may feel the need to care for your body more intentionally. This could be as simple as stretching, eating nourishing foods, or prioritizing rest. The stars remind you that your sensitivity requires balance—when your physical body is supported, your emotional and spiritual energy thrives. Don't push yourself to exhaustion; steady, gentle improvements matter more than drastic changes. Your body is speaking—listen to its wisdom.

Affirmation & Gratitude

I nurture my body with love, honoring its wisdom and needs.

Pisces
28 February 2026

Pisces, today encourages reflection on partnerships and relationships. You may notice where balance has been off, or where harmony flows easily. A conversation could clarify lingering confusion, but honesty is key. Don't shy away from expressing your needs—you deserve reciprocity. For those seeking love, this is a day to set intentions for the type of partner you want to attract. Remember, alignment begins with valuing yourself. Trust that healthy connections naturally follow when you honor your worth.

Affirmation & Gratitude

I attract relationships that reflect balance, respect, and love.

March 2026

Pisces
01 March 2026

A new month begins with a surge of clarity, Pisces. The cosmos highlights your inner wisdom, and you may suddenly see the path ahead more clearly. A project, goal, or dream feels within reach now, provided you focus your energy. Avoid scattering yourself in too many directions. Narrow your intentions and let your actions flow steadily. The universe is nudging you toward progress—trust the timing. Clarity is your ally, and focus is your strength.

Affirmation & Gratitude

I channel my energy into focused action, trusting clarity to guide me.

Pisces
02 March 2026

Pisces, today highlights transformation and release. Something you've been holding onto—whether an outdated belief, a lingering fear, or a physical item—needs to be let go. The universe is clearing space for something greater, but first you must loosen your grip. This isn't loss; it's liberation. Emotions may surface, but lean into them—they're signposts pointing toward healing. Trust that what leaves your life makes space for deeper alignment. The lighter you travel, the freer you become.

Affirmation & Gratitude

I release what no longer serves me, opening my heart to transformation.

Pisces
03 March 2026

Today's energy sparks curiosity and exploration, Pisces. You may feel inspired to learn, travel, or connect with different perspectives. Even a small adventure—like trying new food, exploring nature, or diving into a new subject—can awaken fresh insights. Conversations with others may expand your understanding, reminding you of the vastness of possibility. Growth comes when you step outside your comfort zone, even in subtle ways. Be open to experiences that broaden your spirit.

Affirmation & Gratitude

I welcome new experiences and expand my horizons with curiosity and joy.

Pisces
04 March 2026

Pisces, the stars highlight career and purpose today. You may feel clearer about your calling or notice recognition for your efforts. If work feels stagnant, this is a day to re-evaluate whether your current path aligns with your values. Don't fear change; stepping toward authenticity is always worthwhile. You have unique gifts to share, and the world benefits when you embrace them fully. A conversation with a mentor or colleague could offer validation.

Affirmation & Gratitude

I step confidently toward my purpose, knowing my work carries meaning.

Pisces
05 March 2026

Pisces, today's cosmic influence draws you inward, highlighting reflection and self-discovery. You may feel a little quieter than usual, preferring to observe rather than act. This isn't avoidance—it's wisdom. By stepping back, you allow clarity to surface naturally. Spiritual practices such as meditation, journaling, or even mindful silence are powerful tools today. Don't feel guilty for slowing down; this pause is necessary to realign your energy. A dream or intuitive nudge could hold guidance—trust it, even if it seems subtle.

Affirmation & Gratitude

I honor stillness as a source of wisdom and clarity.

Pisces
06 March 2026

Pisces, today's energy encourages you to embrace community and connection. Friends or colleagues may reach out, offering opportunities for collaboration or simply reminding you of the joy of shared experiences. Don't isolate yourself; your compassionate presence uplifts others. At the same time, ensure you're not giving more than you can sustain. Balance connection with self-care. Networking now could lead to surprising opportunities down the road, so keep your heart and mind open.

Affirmation & Gratitude

I welcome meaningful connections that inspire and support my journey.

Pisces
07 March 2026

Pisces, your ruling planet Neptune heightens your sensitivity today, making you extra receptive to subtle energies around you. While this enhances your intuition, it may also leave you feeling drained if you're not careful. Ground yourself with simple rituals—walk in nature, focus on your breath, or practice gratitude. Use your heightened awareness to channel creativity or spiritual insight. Pay attention to coincidences—they're actually synchronicities guiding you. What feels like chance may in fact be divine timing.

Affirmation & Gratitude

I trust synchronicities as signs that guide me on my path.

Pisces
08 March 2026

Pisces, today's energy is about focus and determination. The cosmos urges you to take concrete steps toward your goals, even if small. While you're often guided by inspiration, consistency ensures progress. Avoid scattering your attention—choose one priority and dedicate yourself fully. A sense of accomplishment will fuel your motivation. Remember, dreams become reality when supported by discipline. This is a day to prove to yourself that you can balance vision with practical follow-through.

Affirmation & Gratitude

I commit to steady progress, knowing small steps lead to big achievements.

Pisces
09 March 2026

Today highlights relationships, Pisces. Someone close to you may need your empathy, or you might feel called to share your heart more openly. Vulnerability deepens connections now, so don't hold back out of fear. At the same time, ensure your compassion doesn't slip into self-sacrifice. Healthy boundaries allow your love to shine without depletion. Whether romantic or platonic, conversations today can create greater harmony and mutual understanding. Love, in all forms, is amplified under today's sky.

Affirmation & Gratitude

I open my heart with honesty, while honoring healthy boundaries.

Pisces
10 March 2026

Pisces, the Moon's influence highlights your need for rest and restoration. If you've been pushing hard, today is your reminder to slow down. Your body and mind will thank you for listening. Take a nap, enjoy a nourishing meal, or retreat into quiet comfort. Renewal comes when you allow yourself permission to pause. Don't mistake rest for laziness—it's part of your rhythm. By honoring your cycles, you become more resilient when challenges arise.

Affirmation & Gratitude

I rest with intention, knowing renewal strengthens my spirit.

Pisces
11 March 2026

The cosmos encourages expansion today, Pisces. You may feel restless or inspired to step outside your comfort zone. Travel, study, or even a simple new experience could spark joy and growth. Curiosity is your compass—follow it. Don't let fear of the unknown hold you back; opportunities often lie just beyond familiar shores. A teacher, mentor, or inspiring story could shift your perspective in powerful ways. Embrace the adventure life offers you now.

Affirmation & Gratitude

I welcome growth and adventure, trusting curiosity to guide me.

Pisces
12 March 2026

Pisces, today's cosmic influence encourages you to revisit your dreams and intentions. Something you once longed for may resurface, reminding you that your desires hold timeless value. Ask yourself: do these goals still resonate with the person you are becoming? If yes, recommit with fresh energy. If not, bless them and release. Reflection today brings clarity, while planning ensures progress. Don't underestimate the power of writing your visions down—the act of committing them to paper amplifies manifestation.

Affirmation & Gratitude

I honor my dreams, trusting the universe to align me with what is right for me now.

Pisces
13 March 2026

Pisces, the Moon highlights your emotional world today, stirring nostalgia or heightened sensitivity. Old wounds may surface, but they appear now so you can finally heal them. Don't avoid these feelings—give them space and compassion. Healing may come through a conversation, journaling, or simply allowing tears to flow. This isn't weakness—it's renewal. Your capacity for empathy grows stronger when you nurture your own heart. Today is about emotional release that clears space for love and joy.

Affirmation & Gratitude

I allow myself to feel fully, knowing emotions guide me toward healing.

Pisces
14 March 2026

Today, Pisces, your intuition feels especially strong, as though you can sense what others are thinking before they speak. While this gift is powerful, use discernment—don't absorb energy that isn't yours. Channel your heightened awareness into creativity or spiritual practices. If confusion arises, trust your gut over external noise. Avoid overanalyzing, as clarity lies in subtle impressions. Pay attention to small signs—the universe may be sending nudges that affirm you're on the right path.

Affirmation & Gratitude

I trust my inner guidance and honor the wisdom my intuition offers me.

Pisces
15 March 2026

Pisces, the stars highlight relationships today. Harmony can be deepened by listening more than speaking, allowing space for others' truths. A loved one may reveal something important, or you may realize it's time to express your own needs more clearly. Balance is the theme—don't fall into over-giving, but don't withdraw either. Love grows when honesty and compassion flow together. This is also a good day for compromise, but not at the cost of self-respect.

Affirmation & Gratitude

I give and receive love in balance, honoring both myself and others equally.

Pisces
16 March 2026

Today highlights your daily routines and wellbeing, Pisces. You may feel the urge to bring more order to your schedule or tend to your health. Focus on small, sustainable shifts—too much change at once may overwhelm you. Pay attention to your body's signals; they reveal what needs care. Practical steps now strengthen your foundation for bigger dreams later. Treat your daily life as sacred—every action contributes to your overall harmony.

Affirmation & Gratitude

I honor my body and routines, creating balance in both small and meaningful ways.

Pisces
17 March 2026

Pisces, today's energy is expansive, encouraging you to explore new horizons. Whether through travel, study, or conversation, growth is available if you step beyond your comfort zone. Your natural curiosity is heightened, making this a wonderful day for learning. Seek inspiration from mentors, books, or experiences that challenge your perspective. The world is offering you a glimpse of its vastness—embrace it with wonder. Don't underestimate how one new idea could change your trajectory.

Affirmation & Gratitude

I welcome growth and exploration, knowing each step expands my spirit.

Pisces
18 March 2026

Pisces, the cosmos turns your attention to career and long-term purpose today. You may feel clearer about your next professional steps or receive recognition for past efforts. If you've been questioning your path, clarity emerges now. Don't be afraid to step into leadership roles—you are capable of more than you realize. Align your ambitions with your values to ensure lasting fulfillment. Progress comes when you trust both your intuition and your discipline to guide you forward.

Affirmation & Gratitude

I align my work with my values, stepping into purpose with confidence.

Pisces
19 March 2026

Pisces, today the cosmic energy emphasizes reflection and inner wisdom. You may feel quieter than usual, sensing the need to pause before making decisions. This is a day for contemplation rather than action. Trust that stepping back allows greater clarity to surface. Spiritual practices are especially potent now—meditation, prayer, or simply sitting in silence could bring profound insights. Avoid rushing or forcing outcomes; patience is your ally. Answers are forming in the background, waiting for the right moment to reveal themselves.

Affirmation & Gratitude

I trust the wisdom of patience, knowing clarity arrives in divine timing.

Pisces
20 March 2026

The Sun shifts into Aries today, Pisces, illuminating your second house of values and resources. This marks the start of a cycle focused on self-worth, finances, and material stability. You may feel motivated to create stronger foundations for your dreams, whether through budgeting, new income opportunities, or recognizing your own value in relationships and work. The universe asks you to take ownership of your worth—it sets the tone for what you allow into your life.

Affirmation & Gratitude

I honor my worth and create stability that supports my dreams.

Pisces
21 March 2026

Pisces, today the Moon highlights communication, making it an excellent day to speak your truth. Conversations may feel healing and clarifying, offering a chance to strengthen relationships or resolve misunderstandings. Writing, journaling, or public speaking are favored, as your words carry extra resonance now. Be mindful not to overexplain—simplicity often conveys the deepest truths. Pay attention also to messages that arrive unexpectedly; the universe may be speaking through others.

Affirmation & Gratitude

I express my truth with clarity, trusting my words to inspire and heal.

Pisces
22 March 2026

The stars turn your attention toward home and emotional security today, Pisces. You may feel drawn to spend more time in your personal space, rearranging, cleaning, or simply enjoying comfort. Family interactions could be highlighted—whether supportive or requiring patience. This is a good day to nurture your roots and strengthen the foundation you stand on. By creating peace at home, you align yourself with greater balance in the outside world.

Affirmation & Gratitude

I nurture my home and heart, creating peace from the inside out.

Pisces
23 March 2026

Pisces, today brings expansive energy that pushes you to explore beyond familiar boundaries. Whether through learning, travel, or connecting with different perspectives, opportunities for growth are everywhere. Don't be afraid to try something new—it could spark inspiration that changes your course. Keep an open mind and embrace curiosity as your guide. Even a small adventure today can ripple into big changes later. The universe is inviting you to broaden your horizons.

Affirmation & Gratitude

I welcome new experiences with openness, trusting growth flows through exploration.

Pisces
24 March 2026

Career and purpose are in the spotlight today, Pisces. You may receive recognition for your efforts or feel clearer about your next professional step. This is a day to think long-term—what do you want to build, and does it align with your soul's truth? Leadership opportunities may present themselves, even if subtly. Don't shy away from them; you're more capable than you realize. Align action with your values, and success will follow.

Affirmation & Gratitude

I step into purpose with confidence, knowing my work holds meaning.

Pisces
25 March 2026

Pisces, today's lunar eclipse stirs deep emotions, bringing hidden truths to the surface. You may feel intense release around relationships, old wounds, or limiting beliefs. While it may feel heavy in the moment, trust that this clearing is essential for your growth. Eclipse energy is transformative—it strips away what no longer serves, leaving space for renewal. Honor your emotions, but don't cling to the past. What leaves now makes way for a brighter path.

Affirmation & Gratitude

I release the past with love, opening myself to transformation and renewal.

Pisces
26 March 2026

Pisces, the energy today feels lighter after yesterday's eclipse intensity. You may notice a sense of relief, as though a weight has been lifted. While clarity might not arrive all at once, trust that the universe has shifted something in your favor. Focus on grounding yourself—spend time in nature, eat nourishing foods, and rest if needed. This is a day to integrate rather than act. Pay attention to subtle signs; they may reveal what's beginning to unfold.

Affirmation & Gratitude

I embrace the calm after change, trusting that renewal is unfolding in my life.

Pisces
27 March 2026

Pisces, today's cosmic energy highlights your relationships. Conversations may feel deeper than usual, offering healing or clarity around old misunderstandings. Someone may reveal a truth that shifts how you see them, or you may feel compelled to share your own heart more openly. Vulnerability is strength now; it clears space for genuine connection. Don't avoid difficult topics—lean into honesty, even if it feels uncomfortable. Trust that truth creates stronger foundations.

Affirmation & Gratitude

I welcome honesty in my relationships, knowing truth strengthens connection.

Pisces
28 March 2026

Pisces, your intuition feels sharp today, almost prophetic. You may pick up on subtle details others miss, guiding you toward wise choices. Use this energy to reflect on long-term plans or creative projects—you'll see what needs adjustment. Spiritual practices are especially potent now; meditation, tarot, or dream work could offer profound insights. Don't second-guess your instincts—they are guiding you toward alignment. The more you trust your inner compass, the clearer your path becomes.

Affirmation & Gratitude

I trust my intuition to guide me with wisdom and clarity.

Pisces
29 March 2026

Today highlights practical matters, Pisces, and while your dreamy nature prefers flow, the cosmos urges you to focus on details. Bills, errands, or organization may call your attention, and addressing them brings peace of mind. Avoid procrastination—it only creates stress later. By tending to practical tasks today, you create freedom for creativity and rest tomorrow. Think of it as tending the soil before planting seeds. Small, steady actions are your allies now.

Affirmation & Gratitude

I handle practical matters with ease, knowing they support my freedom.

Pisces
30 March 2026

Pisces, today you may feel the urge to step out of your comfort zone. The stars highlight growth through new experiences, whether through travel, learning, or simply saying yes to an invitation. Inspiration often comes from unfamiliar places—be open to what arises. A mentor, book, or conversation could shift your perspective. Don't cling to the familiar when adventure calls. You're being nudged to expand your world, one step at a time.

Affirmation & Gratitude

I welcome new horizons, trusting growth flows through adventure.

Pisces
31 March 2026

Career and purpose are spotlighted today, Pisces. You may receive recognition for past efforts or feel a surge of motivation to pursue your goals more directly. Ask yourself: does my current path reflect who I am becoming? If not, small adjustments can redirect your energy. Don't underestimate your ability to lead—your quiet wisdom is an asset. Take a step toward your long-term vision, even if small. The universe supports aligned action.

Affirmation & Gratitude

I take confident steps toward my true purpose, trusting my path.

April
2026

Pisces
01 April 2026

Pisces, today opens with fresh energy, offering a sense of renewal. You may feel inspired to set intentions for the month ahead, focusing on what you want to grow. The cosmos encourages clarity and commitment—dreams need structure to thrive. Avoid scattering yourself in too many directions; choose a few priorities and dedicate yourself fully. This is also a great day for creativity, as your imagination flows easily. Let vision and action work hand in hand.

Affirmation & Gratitude

I set clear intentions, blending vision with action to manifest my dreams.

Pisces
02 April 2026

Pisces, today the cosmos highlights your finances and sense of self-worth. You may feel nudged to review your budget, savings, or spending habits. This isn't about restriction but empowerment—aligning money with your values brings peace. You could also notice an opportunity for growth, whether through a new income source or a fresh perspective on abundance. Remember, prosperity is both material and spiritual. Gratitude attracts more of what you seek, so focus on what's working instead of lack.

Affirmation & Gratitude

I align my resources with gratitude, knowing abundance flows naturally into my life.

Pisces
03 April 2026

Pisces, communication is key today. The Moon encourages heartfelt conversations, and you may feel inspired to speak your truth or listen deeply to another. Pay attention to the tone of your words; compassion ensures they are received well. Writing, journaling, or even creating poetry could feel especially fulfilling now. You may also receive an important message that feels perfectly timed. Trust that today's exchanges carry guidance and clarity, helping you move forward with confidence.

Affirmation & Gratitude

I communicate with clarity and kindness, trusting my words to create connection.

Pisces
04 April 2026

Your emotional world is highlighted today, Pisces. You may feel nostalgic or find yourself revisiting memories that stir strong feelings. Instead of resisting, honor these emotions—they're part of your healing journey. Family or home matters could surface, offering a chance to resolve tension or deepen bonds. Create a safe space for yourself, whether through cozy comforts, rest, or spiritual rituals. Emotional release today makes way for renewed energy tomorrow. Let feelings flow without judgment.

Affirmation & Gratitude

I honor my emotions as part of my healing, allowing love to flow freely.

Pisces
05 April 2026

Pisces, today is about expansion and exploration. You may feel drawn to study, travel, or dive into spiritual practices that broaden your perspective. The cosmos encourages curiosity—don't shy away from new experiences, even small ones. Growth doesn't always mean grand gestures; sometimes it's found in a new book, a conversation, or a simple change of routine. Follow the spark of curiosity and let it lead you to fresh inspiration and wisdom.

Affirmation & Gratitude

I embrace curiosity as a path to growth and new possibilities.

Pisces
06 April 2026

Pisces, your career and purpose come into focus today. You may feel recognition for your efforts, or clarity may arrive about your next step. Ask yourself: does your current path align with your deepest values? If not, it may be time for adjustments. Don't fear change—your talents are ready to shine in new ways. The universe supports steady, authentic effort. Take a step, however small, that moves you closer to your true purpose.

Affirmation & Gratitude

I align my work with my soul's truth, taking steps toward lasting fulfillment.

Pisces
07 April 2026

Pisces, today the cosmos invites you to slow down and restore. After recent demands, your spirit may crave quiet and reflection. Don't ignore this need—rest is just as important as action. Spiritual practices like meditation, journaling, or simply sitting in silence will replenish you. If dreams feel vivid, pay attention—they carry guidance from your subconscious. Allow yourself to retreat without guilt; you emerge stronger when you honor your cycles of energy.

Affirmation & Gratitude

I restore my spirit through rest, trusting stillness as part of my path.

Pisces
08 April 2026

Pisces, today's solar eclipse is a powerful turning point. This energy activates your second house of values and resources, bringing revelations about self-worth, money, and stability. You may suddenly realize where you've undervalued yourself or relied on shaky foundations. While change may feel intense, trust that it's clearing the way for alignment. Release scarcity thinking and embrace your worth—you are capable of attracting security and abundance. This eclipse begins a cycle of empowerment that unfolds over months ahead.

Affirmation & Gratitude

I embrace change with courage, knowing my worth attracts abundance and stability.

Pisces
09 April 2026

Pisces, today the energy begins to settle after yesterday's eclipse, though you may still feel emotionally raw or uncertain. Give yourself time to integrate changes. Journaling, rest, and grounding activities will help you process what has shifted. Avoid rushing into decisions just yet—clarity will come with patience. Trust that the universe is gently guiding you toward greater alignment with your true worth. This is a day for self-care and reflection, not major action.

Affirmation & Gratitude

I give myself grace and patience as I integrate new clarity into my life.

Pisces
10 April 2026

Pisces, the Moon stirs your communication sector, making conversations lively and meaningful. You may feel inspired to share your story or speak openly about what's been on your mind. Others are more receptive now, so honesty can build bridges. At the same time, be mindful of overextending—listening is just as powerful as speaking. Writing or journaling could also bring clarity. Messages from the universe may arrive through synchronicities or casual conversations.

Affirmation & Gratitude

I express myself with honesty and listen deeply to the wisdom around me.

Pisces
11 April 2026

Pisces, home and family come into focus today. You may feel drawn to nurture your environment or create more harmony in your space. Emotional matters within family or close relationships could arise, offering opportunities for healing. Don't shy away from addressing them—your compassion can ease tension. Small acts, like rearranging a room or cooking a comforting meal, carry big impact. By tending to your foundation, you create stability that supports every other area of life.

Affirmation & Gratitude

I create harmony in my home, knowing peace within supports peace without.

Pisces
12 April 2026

Pisces, today's cosmic energy urges you to explore beyond the familiar. You may crave adventure, learning, or a fresh perspective. Even if travel isn't possible, expand your mind through books, documentaries, or conversation with someone from a different background. This is also a great day to lean into spiritual growth. The more you open yourself to new wisdom, the more aligned your path becomes. Curiosity is your compass—follow it without hesitation.

Affirmation & Gratitude

I welcome new perspectives that expand my spirit and inspire my journey.

Pisces
13 April 2026

Pisces, your career and reputation may feel highlighted today, with opportunities to shine or receive recognition for your work. Even small achievements won't go unnoticed. If you've been uncertain about your direction, clarity begins to form. The cosmos supports you in taking practical steps toward your goals. Don't shy away from responsibility—your quiet leadership is valued more than you realize. Aligning your work with your values ensures long-term fulfillment.

Affirmation & Gratitude

I step confidently into purpose, trusting my path unfolds with meaning.

Pisces
14 April 2026

Pisces, today invites you to slow down and turn inward. After recent busyness, your spirit needs time to reflect and reset. Dreams may feel vivid, carrying messages from your subconscious. Pay attention—they could hold guidance for your next steps. This is not a day for rushing; instead, lean into stillness and spiritual practices. Journaling, meditation, or a walk in nature will restore balance. Solitude today is deeply healing, not isolating.

Affirmation & Gratitude

I embrace solitude and reflection, knowing stillness renews my spirit.

Pisces
15 April 2026

Pisces, today's energy is transformative. You may feel called to release what no longer serves you, whether an outdated habit, relationship pattern, or lingering doubt. The universe is offering you the strength to let go and trust the process of renewal. Emotional release may feel intense but is necessary to make space for growth. Transformation often feels like endings, but they're simply the beginning of something greater. Trust that what leaves now clears the way for light.

Affirmation & Gratitude

I release with courage, trusting transformation to guide me toward growth.

Pisces
16 April 2026

Pisces, today the cosmos shines a light on relationships and partnerships. You may feel more aware of the dynamics between giving and receiving. If balance has been missing, this is the time to address it with honesty and kindness. Conversations may feel more intimate, offering opportunities to strengthen bonds. If single, you may recognize patterns you're ready to release before stepping into something new. Trust that authentic connection comes when you honor your own needs first.

Affirmation & Gratitude

I welcome balanced connections that honor both my needs and those of others.

Pisces
17 April 2026

Pisces, today your energy is drawn toward daily routines, health, and responsibilities. While not glamorous, these areas create the stability you need for your dreams. Pay attention to small habits—they either build you up or wear you down. A small shift, like organizing your day differently or focusing on wellbeing, could make a big difference. Avoid overwhelm by taking things step by step. Discipline paired with compassion creates progress without burnout.

Affirmation & Gratitude

I nurture my wellbeing through steady habits that support my body, mind, and spirit.

Pisces
18 April 2026

Pisces, today's cosmic flow encourages you to expand your horizons. Curiosity is high—you may crave learning, adventure, or exploring fresh ideas. Travel, study, or spiritual exploration may call you. Inspiration often comes when you step outside routine, so allow yourself to try something new. Even a small shift, like reading a book in a different genre, can spark insight. Growth is waiting, but you must answer the call.

Affirmation & Gratitude

I embrace curiosity as a guide, opening myself to new wisdom and growth.

Pisces
19 April 2026

Pisces, today the Sun shifts into Taurus, highlighting your communication sector. Over the weeks ahead, you'll be called to use your voice more—whether through conversations, writing, or teaching. Today may bring a glimpse of that energy. Words carry power, so speak with clarity and intention. Someone may reach out with news that shifts your perspective. Be open, but remember that listening is equally important. Your voice and your silence both hold weight.

Affirmation & Gratitude

I use my words with intention, trusting my voice to create clarity and connection.

Pisces
20 April 2026

Pisces, today draws attention to home and family matters. You may feel the need to nurture your space or revisit old emotional patterns tied to your roots. Healing conversations with family may unfold, or you may choose to simply create harmony in your personal sanctuary. A safe, comfortable environment is your foundation for thriving in the wider world. Take time today to anchor yourself in comfort and love.

Affirmation & Gratitude

I create peace within my home and honor the roots that support me.

Pisces
21 April 2026

Pisces, today the stars highlight expansion through curiosity and exploration. Conversations with others may spark new insights or lead you to explore topics you hadn't considered. This is an excellent day for learning, research, or seeking mentorship. Don't dismiss small nudges—they may open big doors. The universe is encouraging you to broaden your mind and look at possibilities from fresh angles. Keep curiosity alive; it's your compass today.

Affirmation & Gratitude

I welcome fresh ideas and allow curiosity to guide me toward growth.

Pisces
22 April 2026

Pisces, today's Full Moon in Scorpio brings intensity and transformation. Emotions may run deep, revealing truths you've been avoiding. This lunation highlights your spiritual growth, travel, or learning path, asking you to release outdated beliefs. Transformation can feel heavy, but it's necessary for expansion. Trust that what feels like an ending is clearing space for wisdom and renewal. Allow yourself to feel deeply, but don't cling—release is liberation.

Affirmation & Gratitude

I release limiting beliefs, opening myself to transformation and higher truth.

Pisces
23 April 2026

Pisces, the energy after yesterday's Full Moon may feel raw, but it also brings clarity. You're beginning to see what no longer serves you, and that realization is liberating. Today is ideal for integration—processing what surfaced and choosing how to move forward. Avoid rushing; instead, focus on grounding yourself in gentle routines. A walk in nature, journaling, or even mindful breathing can help you settle. Transformation takes time, but every step creates space for new beginnings.

Affirmation & Gratitude

I allow transformation to unfold gently, trusting each step brings me closer to alignment.

Pisces
24 April 2026

Pisces, communication feels emphasized today, with opportunities for heartfelt conversations or written expression. You may find yourself sharing something personal, or someone close may open up to you. Listening deeply creates healing for both of you. Avoid gossip or scattering your words—speak only what feels true and necessary. Your intuition guides your communication now, making your voice especially impactful. Writing, teaching, or journaling may reveal insights you hadn't yet acknowledged.

Affirmation & Gratitude

I speak and listen with compassion, allowing my words to carry healing energy.

Pisces
25 April 2026

Pisces, today's focus is on home, family, and emotional security. You may feel called to nurture your living space or spend quality time with loved ones. A memory or family issue could resurface, but it's an opportunity to create closure or deeper understanding. Creating harmony within your environment allows you to feel stronger in the outside world. Small acts—like cleaning, rearranging, or cooking—can become grounding rituals that bring peace.

Affirmation & Gratitude

I nurture my home and family with love, creating harmony within and around me.

Pisces
26 April 2026

Pisces, today brings curiosity and expansion. You may feel drawn to explore new ideas, cultures, or spiritual teachings. A conversation could inspire you to shift your perspective or consider new possibilities. Don't dismiss the pull to learn—your growth thrives on curiosity. Even a small act of exploration today can have long-term ripple effects. Let inspiration guide you and be open to experiences that broaden your worldview.

Affirmation & Gratitude

I welcome new knowledge and allow curiosity to expand my spirit.

Pisces
27 April 2026

Pisces, your career and long-term goals take the spotlight today. Recognition for your work may come your way, or you may feel a surge of motivation to pursue ambitions with renewed focus. Ask yourself: does your current direction align with your values and soul's truth? If not, today provides clarity about adjustments needed. Trust that even small steps toward authenticity can bring powerful results.

Affirmation & Gratitude

I align my ambitions with my values, building a purposeful future.

Pisces
28 April 2026

Pisces, today highlights rest, reflection, and spiritual connection. You may feel the need to retreat from busyness and honor your inner world. This isn't withdrawal—it's restoration. Spend time in meditation, journaling, or connecting with nature. Insights may arrive in stillness, especially through dreams or synchronicities. Give yourself permission to step back without guilt. You emerge stronger when you honor your cycles of rest and renewal.

Affirmation & Gratitude

I restore my spirit in stillness, allowing wisdom to rise within me.

Pisces
29 April 2026

Pisces, today the cosmos encourages transformation. You may feel called to release old patterns, fears, or habits that keep you from your full potential. While letting go may feel uncomfortable, trust that it's making way for growth. Emotional depth runs high, but facing it courageously brings healing. Transformation is rarely easy, yet it always brings you closer to your truth. Allow yourself to shed what no longer belongs.

Affirmation & Gratitude

I release what no longer serves, stepping into transformation with courage and trust.

Pisces
30 April 2026

Pisces, the month closes with an emphasis on clarity and communication. You may feel inspired to share your thoughts openly, or you could receive important news that shifts your perspective. This is also a powerful day for journaling or setting intentions around how you want to express yourself in the months ahead. Words carry power—use them carefully. Honest conversations can clear confusion, strengthen relationships, and create forward momentum. Speak from your heart, and others will listen.

Affirmation & Gratitude

I express myself with honesty and clarity, trusting my words to create positive change.

May
2026

Pisces
01 May 2026

Pisces, May begins with energy focused on grounding and self-worth. You may feel nudged to look at how you value yourself and whether your actions reflect that. Financial matters could come into focus—budgeting, saving, or rethinking priorities. Instead of seeing this as restrictive, frame it as empowerment. You are building foundations for the abundance you deserve. Trust that security grows from honoring your worth, both emotionally and materially.

Affirmation & Gratitude

I honor my worth and create stability that supports my dreams.

Pisces
02 May 2026

Pisces, today highlights curiosity and exploration. You may feel inspired to learn something new, study, or explore a subject that has always intrigued you. Even a conversation could open new pathways of thought. The cosmos encourages you to broaden your mind and embrace experiences that challenge old beliefs. Growth thrives on openness, so lean into opportunities to expand. A mentor, book, or even synchronicity may guide you toward wisdom.

Affirmation & Gratitude

I welcome growth and learning, allowing curiosity to expand my perspective.

Pisces
03 May 2026

Pisces, your career or public life may come into focus today. Recognition for your hard work could arrive, or you may feel called to step into greater responsibility. If you've been doubting your path, clarity is emerging now. Align your ambitions with what feels authentic rather than what others expect. A small but deliberate step toward your purpose today could have a long-lasting impact. Trust yourself—you're more capable than you realize.

Affirmation & Gratitude

I step confidently into my purpose, aligning my work with my soul's truth.

Pisces
04 May 2026

Pisces, today invites you to rest and reflect. After recent focus on outer responsibilities, your inner world calls for attention. Give yourself permission to retreat, meditate, or simply enjoy quiet time. Spiritual insights may surface, reminding you of the importance of balance between doing and being. Avoid overcommitting socially; solitude will be deeply restorative now. In stillness, clarity and peace can rise naturally.

Affirmation & Gratitude

I honor rest as sacred, knowing stillness restores my strength.

Pisces
05 May 2026

Pisces, today's New Moon in Taurus activates your communication sector, offering a fresh start around how you express yourself. This is a powerful time to set intentions for writing, learning, or conversations you want to pursue. You may feel inspired to begin a project that involves your voice—whether spoken or written. The universe supports new beginnings here, so don't hold back. Your words matter more than you realize.

Affirmation & Gratitude

I set new intentions for honest, inspired communication that reflects my truth.

Pisces
06 May 2026

Pisces, today's energy feels light and expansive, encouraging connection with others. Conversations flow easily, and you may feel more social than usual. This is a great day for networking, catching up with friends, or simply enjoying company. Collaboration could lead to surprising opportunities, so stay open. At the same time, remember to balance connection with self-care—don't give more than you comfortably can. Joy and laughter uplift your spirit today.

Affirmation & Gratitude

I welcome joyful connections that inspire and support me.

Pisces
07 May 2026

Pisces, today your emotional world feels heightened, as the Moon stirs memories and sensitivities. Old feelings may resurface, perhaps triggered by a conversation or familiar place. Instead of resisting them, embrace these emotions—they carry messages about what still needs healing or closure. You may feel drawn to retreat into the comfort of home or spend time with loved ones. Allow nurturing energy to surround you and remember that release is part of renewal.

Affirmation & Gratitude

I embrace my emotions with compassion, knowing they guide me toward healing.

Pisces
08 May 2026

Pisces, today highlights curiosity and exploration. You may feel pulled toward study, travel, or simply trying something new. Even small shifts—like engaging with fresh ideas or meeting someone different—can expand your perspective. The universe is encouraging you to say yes to growth, even if it feels uncertain. Inspiration often comes when you're willing to step outside your comfort zone. Allow yourself to be a student of life today.

Affirmation & Gratitude

I welcome new experiences with openness, trusting they lead me to growth.

Pisces
09 May 2026

Pisces, your career and public life are highlighted today. You may feel motivated to focus on your goals or take practical steps toward advancement. Recognition for your efforts could arrive, or a new opportunity may appear. Ask yourself if your ambitions align with your deeper values—success feels sweeter when it matches your soul's truth. Don't shy away from responsibility; your quiet determination is noticed more than you realize.

Affirmation & Gratitude

I pursue my goals with integrity, aligning ambition with purpose.

Pisces
10 May 2026

Pisces, today the cosmos encourages rest and reflection. After recent busyness, your spirit needs time to restore. Solitude, meditation, or journaling will help clear your mind and recharge your energy. Don't feel guilty for stepping back—it's necessary for balance. You may also find that inspiration arrives in the quiet moments when you're not trying to force outcomes. Today is for inner peace and gentle renewal.

Affirmation & Gratitude

I honor stillness and allow peace to restore my spirit.

Pisces
11 May 2026

Pisces, today's energy brings transformation. You may feel ready to release a pattern, belief, or relationship dynamic that has weighed you down. Though change can feel unsettling, trust that this is an opening for growth. Emotional honesty with yourself is key—acknowledge what you've outgrown and take a step toward freedom. Transformation today may feel subtle but will ripple into the future in profound ways.

Affirmation & Gratitude

I release the old with courage, making space for renewal and growth.

Pisces
12 May 2026

Pisces, today highlights friendships and community. You may feel more social, craving connection with like-minded souls. Group activities, collaborations, or even casual conversations could uplift and inspire you. Surround yourself with those who share your vision and values—together, you amplify each other's light. Be mindful not to give too much of your energy away; balance support with self-care. This is a day to celebrate connection and shared purpose.

Affirmation & Gratitude

I value uplifting friendships and welcome community that inspires me.

Pisces
13 May 2026

Pisces, today's energy turns inward again, urging reflection. You may feel quieter, sensing the need to pause before making decisions. Spiritual practices will feel especially nourishing—dream work, meditation, or journaling may reveal insights. Don't dismiss subtle nudges; your intuition is guiding you now. Avoid overcommitting socially, as solitude holds more power for you today. This is not withdrawal—it's a chance to gather strength and clarity.

Affirmation & Gratitude

I honor reflection, trusting my intuition to guide me forward.

Pisces
14 May 2026

Pisces, today's energy highlights your inner world and subconscious patterns. You may feel more reflective than usual, drawn to examine what beliefs or fears are still shaping your choices. This is a powerful day for journaling or meditation, as insights can surface that help you release old limitations. Don't push for external progress—true movement comes from clearing what holds you back inside. By recognizing these patterns, you step into more authentic freedom.

Affirmation & Gratitude

I release outdated patterns, trusting that inner clarity creates outer growth.

Pisces
15 May 2026

Pisces, today's Full Moon in Taurus illuminates your communication sector. You may feel a strong urge to speak your truth, whether through heartfelt conversations, writing, or creative expression. This lunation supports clarity and closure—something unsaid may finally be voiced, bringing healing and resolution. Be mindful of your words; they carry weight now. Listening is equally important, as others may reveal truths that shift your perspective. Trust the power of expression and understanding.

Affirmation & Gratitude

I express myself with honesty and compassion, allowing words to heal and empower.

Pisces
16 May 2026

Pisces, the energy today encourages grounding and practical focus. After the emotional intensity of yesterday's Full Moon, you may feel the need to stabilize yourself. Tackle small tasks, organize your environment, or care for your body through simple routines. Practical action provides calm and clarity. Don't underestimate how powerful small acts of responsibility can be —they create the structure your dreams need to thrive. Today is about steady progress, not dramatic leaps.

Affirmation & Gratitude

I ground myself through simple, steady actions that support my wellbeing.

Pisces
17 May 2026

Pisces, relationships come into focus today, with opportunities for deeper connection. You may feel called to spend time with someone close or have a heartfelt conversation that clears the air. Balance is key—make sure your giving is matched by receiving. If single, you may notice insights about what you truly want in a partner. Harmony grows through honesty and presence. Allow your compassionate heart to guide interactions without sacrificing your own needs.

Affirmation & Gratitude

I welcome balanced, nurturing relationships that honor both myself and others.

Pisces
18 May 2026

Pisces, today highlights your daily routines and health. You may feel the urge to improve how you manage time, energy, or physical wellbeing. Even small adjustments—like better sleep, mindful eating, or creating order in your schedule—can ripple into long-term benefits. Don't let perfectionism stop you; progress matters more than flawlessness. Treat your body with respect, and it will support you in reaching your bigger dreams.

Affirmation & Gratitude

I nurture my body and routines, honoring the small steps that create long-term harmony.

Pisces
19 May 2026

Pisces, today the stars inspire curiosity and learning. You may feel drawn to study, explore new ideas, or have conversations that expand your worldview. A teacher, mentor, or inspiring story may offer insight that shifts your perspective. Travel, even short-distance, could also be fulfilling. Embrace openness and let your curiosity guide you toward new opportunities for growth. Don't limit yourself to the familiar —life is nudging you to explore further.

Affirmation & Gratitude

I welcome new ideas and experiences, allowing curiosity to expand my horizons.

Pisces
20 May 2026

Pisces, the Sun shifts into Gemini today, highlighting your home and family sector for the weeks ahead. Over this period, you'll be drawn to nurture your roots, strengthen family ties, and create comfort in your living environment. Today, you may already feel the call to connect with loved ones or bring harmony to your space. Remember, home is also within you—create inner peace and it will reflect in your outer world.

Affirmation & Gratitude

I create harmony within myself and in my home, honoring the roots that sustain me.

Pisces
21 May 2026

Pisces, today's energy highlights emotional connections at home and within family. You may feel drawn to nurture your personal environment, creating comfort and stability. A family conversation could arise, offering a chance for healing or deeper understanding. If emotions feel heavy, don't suppress them—address them gently. Domestic harmony supports every other area of your life, so give attention to your roots. Creating peace in your space allows you to move forward with confidence and clarity.

Affirmation & Gratitude

I nurture my home and family, creating a foundation of love and harmony.

Pisces
22 May 2026

Pisces, today the cosmos encourages curiosity and exploration. You may feel restless or eager to step outside of your routine. This is an excellent day for study, short trips, or conversations that expand your perspective. Even small adventures can spark big ideas. Inspiration may arrive through books, mentors, or synchronicities that nudge you toward growth. Follow your intuition and be open to new experiences.

Affirmation & Gratitude

I welcome fresh ideas and new experiences that expand my heart and mind.

Pisces
23 May 2026

Pisces, career and long-term goals come into focus today. You may receive recognition for your work or feel motivated to pursue ambitions more directly. A conversation with a boss, mentor, or colleague may offer insight that helps you see the bigger picture. Ask yourself: are you aligning your actions with your purpose, or are you following a path that no longer inspires you? Today supports taking practical steps toward long-term fulfillment.

Affirmation & Gratitude

I align my goals with my soul's truth, moving forward with purpose.

Pisces
24 May 2026

Pisces, today invites you to retreat and reflect. You may crave solitude, sensing that your energy is best spent in quiet restoration. Pay attention to dreams, as they may hold guidance. This is a day to nurture your inner world, not push outward. Spiritual practices will feel especially powerful now. Don't see rest as weakness—it's fuel for what's ahead. Clarity often arises when you stop forcing answers and allow space for wisdom to surface.

Affirmation & Gratitude

I honor rest and reflection, trusting wisdom to rise in stillness.

Pisces
25 May 2026

Pisces, today's energy brings transformation and release. You may feel the need to let go of a habit, fear, or relationship dynamic that no longer serves you. Though change can feel unsettling, trust that the universe is clearing space for something greater. Emotional intensity may arise, but lean into it—it's a sign of deep healing. This is a day to face truths with courage and open yourself to renewal.

Affirmation & Gratitude

I release the old with love, creating space for transformation and growth.

Pisces
26 May 2026

Pisces, friendships and community connections feel highlighted today. You may feel more social, seeking out the company of those who inspire you. Collaboration is favored—working with others could bring progress and joy. At the same time, notice where connections feel draining and consider where boundaries are needed. Surround yourself with people who uplift your energy. Shared purpose and vision will help you thrive, both personally and professionally.

Affirmation & Gratitude

I value uplifting friendships and create community that supports my spirit.

Pisces
27 May 2026

Pisces, today draws you inward once again. You may feel more reflective, needing time alone to process recent changes. Don't resist this pull—it's an important part of your cycle. Spiritual practices like meditation, journaling, or simply spending time in silence will restore your balance. Dreams may feel especially vivid now, offering guidance from your subconscious. Allow yourself to integrate, recharge, and prepare for the next stage of growth.

Affirmation & Gratitude

I find renewal in solitude, trusting stillness to guide me forward.

Pisces
28 May 2026

Pisces, today the cosmos highlights transformation and hidden truths. You may feel emotions rising from deep within, asking for release. This is not a time to suppress feelings but to allow them to flow, bringing clarity and freedom. Conversations or realizations may surface that reveal what has been hidden. While it may feel intense, remember that endings often pave the way for beginnings. Trust that you're being guided through an important shift, even if the path isn't fully clear yet.

Affirmation & Gratitude

I embrace transformation, trusting that release makes room for renewal.

Pisces
29 May 2026

Pisces, friendships and community take the spotlight today. You may find yourself drawn to spend time with people who inspire and uplift you. Collaboration is favored, and group activities can spark new ideas. Notice which connections feel nourishing and which drain your energy. It may be time to step back from certain dynamics while leaning into those that support your growth. Surround yourself with those who celebrate your authenticity.

Affirmation & Gratitude

I welcome friendships that uplift me and honor the joy of shared connection.

Pisces
30 May 2026

Pisces, today may bring a need for solitude and introspection. Your energy feels quieter, and you may prefer reflection over outward activity. This is an excellent day for meditation, journaling, or simply letting your thoughts wander. Dreams may carry important messages, so keep a notebook handy. Don't feel pressured to socialize or achieve—rest and reflection are productive in their own way. Trust that slowing down is part of your process.

Affirmation & Gratitude

I honor solitude and reflection, allowing wisdom to emerge in stillness.

Pisces
31 May 2026

Pisces, today's energy feels expansive, urging you to look at long-term goals. You may feel a surge of motivation to clarify your vision for the future. Career matters could come into focus, or you may feel inspired to take steps toward your personal purpose. Avoid scattering your energy—choose one or two priorities and commit. Small, consistent action now creates lasting success. The universe supports your ambition when it's aligned with your truth.

Affirmation & Gratitude

I focus my energy on goals that reflect my authentic self.

June

2026

Pisces
01 June 2026

Pisces, the new month opens with attention on your spiritual world. You may feel more intuitive, sensitive, or attuned to signs and synchronicities. Pay close attention to subtle nudges—they are guiding you. This is a powerful day for setting spiritual intentions, beginning a new practice, or deepening meditation. Don't ignore your inner voice; it's leading you toward greater clarity. By honoring your spirit, you set the tone for the month ahead.

Affirmation & Gratitude

I trust my intuition and set intentions that honor my spirit.

Pisces
02 June 2026

Pisces, transformation energy continues to surround you today. You may feel ready to release something that has been weighing heavily—perhaps a belief, habit, or emotional burden. While letting go may feel uncomfortable, it is freeing. Conversations may reveal deeper truths that help you see clearly. The universe asks you to trust the process, knowing you are making room for growth and alignment. Transformation is not loss—it is evolution.

Affirmation & Gratitude

I release with courage, trusting transformation as my guide.

Pisces
03 June 2026

Pisces, today's energy brings friendships, networks, and community to the forefront. Collaborations may thrive, and being around like-minded souls lifts your spirit. You may feel inspired to join a group or reconnect with people who share your values. Be mindful of your energy—give to connections that feel supportive rather than draining. The right community strengthens your confidence and helps you grow. Celebrate the joy of belonging without losing your individuality.

Affirmation & Gratitude

I cherish supportive connections that help me grow while honoring my true self.

Pisces
04 June 2026

Pisces, today's energy is deeply introspective. You may feel the need to step back from the world and spend time in solitude. This isn't withdrawal—it's replenishment. Dreams, meditation, or journaling may reveal truths you've overlooked. If you've been running on empty, today is a reminder to honor your inner world as much as your outer duties. Don't force productivity; wisdom arises in stillness. Allow your spirit to rest, and you'll feel clarity returning in the days ahead.

Affirmation & Gratitude

I honor stillness as sacred, allowing quiet moments to restore and guide me.

Pisces
05 June 2026

Pisces, the cosmos highlights transformation today. Emotional intensity may surface, showing you what is ready to be released. This could be an old pattern, a lingering fear, or even a habit that no longer supports your growth. While the process may feel heavy, trust that the universe is helping you shed what holds you back. Every release creates room for renewal. Allow the emotions to flow—healing lies in acceptance, not resistance.

Affirmation & Gratitude

I release with love, trusting that transformation clears space for new beginnings.

Pisces
06 June 2026

Pisces, community and friendships are in focus today. You may feel more connected to your social circles, or perhaps you'll be drawn to meet new people who share your passions. Collaboration can spark inspiration, and group projects may move forward. Be mindful of your boundaries, though—give where it feels nourishing, not draining. Surround yourself with those who celebrate your authenticity. Collective energy uplifts you now.

Affirmation & Gratitude

I celebrate uplifting friendships and value the joy of community.

Pisces
07 June 2026

Pisces, today may feel quieter, with your energy turned inward. Reflection is favored, and your intuition is heightened. Pay attention to dreams or subtle nudges—they're guiding you toward clarity. Rest may be needed, especially if you've been socially or emotionally stretched. Don't see solitude as isolation; instead, embrace it as sacred time to reconnect with yourself. Spiritual practices feel especially powerful, offering insights that shape your next steps.

Affirmation & Gratitude

I embrace solitude as healing, trusting my intuition to guide me forward.

Pisces
08 June 2026

Pisces, today's energy is expansive, urging you to broaden your horizons. Learning, travel, or exploring new ideas may inspire growth. Conversations with others could introduce fresh perspectives, sparking curiosity and excitement. Don't shy away from opportunities that challenge old ways of thinking—they are leading you toward wisdom. Even small steps into unfamiliar territory today can have long-term benefits. Growth comes from openness and curiosity.

Affirmation & Gratitude

I welcome growth and expansion, trusting curiosity to lead me forward.

Pisces
09 June 2026

Pisces, career and purpose are highlighted today. Recognition for your efforts could come, or you may feel a surge of motivation to realign your ambitions with your true calling. Ask yourself: is the work you're doing fulfilling, or does it feel like a compromise? The cosmos urges you to take practical steps toward purpose-driven success. Trust that your unique talents are needed—they shine brighter when expressed authentically.

Affirmation & Gratitude

I align my work with purpose, trusting my gifts to create impact.

Pisces
10 June 2026

Pisces, today's New Moon in Gemini illuminates your home and family sector, offering fresh beginnings in your personal life. You may feel called to create harmony in your living environment, repair family connections, or set intentions around emotional security. This lunation invites you to build stability that nurtures your soul. Even small actions, like reorganizing your space or reaching out to loved ones, carry powerful impact.

Affirmation & Gratitude

I set intentions for peace and harmony within my home and heart.

Pisces
11 June 2026

Pisces, the days following the New Moon bring clarity around your home and emotional foundation. You may feel called to prioritize family, nurture your space, or create more stability in your private life. Old patterns tied to your roots may surface, offering opportunities for healing. Trust that the more peaceful your inner and outer environment, the easier it is for you to thrive in the wider world. A secure base allows your dreams to grow stronger.

Affirmation & Gratitude

I create peace in my home and heart, knowing both are sacred foundations.

Pisces
12 June 2026

Pisces, today the cosmos emphasizes curiosity and expansion. You may crave learning, travel, or engaging in conversations that inspire fresh thinking. Inspiration may arrive through a mentor, a book, or even a chance encounter. Pay attention to where your curiosity is leading you—it may be pointing you toward your next opportunity. This is also an excellent day to revisit long-term goals and see where a fresh perspective can breathe new life into them.

Affirmation & Gratitude

I follow curiosity with openness, trusting it leads me toward growth and wisdom.

Pisces
13 June 2026

Pisces, your career and ambitions come into focus today. Recognition for your efforts may arrive, or you may feel driven to pursue your goals with renewed focus. Don't ignore inner nudges if they're guiding you toward change—this is the time to realign your path with your deeper purpose. A practical step today, no matter how small, can ripple into meaningful progress. Remember, your talents are unique and deserve to be shared.

Affirmation & Gratitude

I take steps toward my true calling, aligning ambition with purpose.

Pisces
14 June 2026

Pisces, today invites reflection and introspection. You may crave solitude, sensing the need to recharge and gather your thoughts. Don't dismiss this urge—rest is a vital part of your rhythm. Meditation, journaling, or time in nature will bring clarity and calm. Insights may surface that help you see your path more clearly. This is not a day for rushing forward; it's a day for listening inward.

Affirmation & Gratitude

I honor stillness and reflection, trusting wisdom arises in quiet moments.

Pisces
15 June 2026

Pisces, transformation is in the air today. Emotional intensity may surface, asking you to release something that no longer serves your growth. This could be an old belief, a fear, or even a relationship dynamic. Though the process may feel heavy, it's opening the door to freedom and alignment. Trust the universe is clearing space for renewal. Lean into the emotions—they are showing you where healing is ready to happen.

Affirmation & Gratitude

I release the old with courage, creating space for transformation and renewal.

Pisces
16 June 2026

Pisces, friendships and community come into focus today. You may feel drawn to connect with like-minded people who uplift and inspire you. Group activities or collaborations may be especially fulfilling, sparking ideas and joy. Pay attention to which connections energize you and which feel draining—it's time to align your social circle with your values. The right community strengthens your confidence and sense of belonging.

Affirmation & Gratitude

I cherish uplifting connections that inspire and support my growth.

Pisces
17 June 2026

Pisces, today's energy feels quieter, guiding you inward. You may feel more sensitive than usual, needing time to retreat and restore. Don't ignore this call; solitude today will bring renewal. Dreams may feel vivid, carrying messages from your subconscious. Reflect on them—they may hold guidance for your path ahead. This is a day for spiritual practices, gentle self-care, and honoring your need for peace.

Affirmation & Gratitude

I find renewal in solitude, trusting rest strengthens my spirit.

Pisces
18 June 2026

Pisces, today's cosmic energy is expansive, encouraging you to look beyond the familiar. You may feel inspired to study, explore, or connect with new perspectives. Even small experiences—like reading a thought-provoking book, attending a workshop, or speaking with someone from a different background—can broaden your worldview. This is also a wonderful day for spiritual practices that help you see life from a higher vantage point. Embrace curiosity, as it will lead to growth and fresh inspiration.

Affirmation & Gratitude

I welcome curiosity as my guide, opening myself to wisdom and new experiences.

Pisces
19 June 2026

Pisces, your career and ambitions come into focus today. Recognition may arrive, or you may feel motivated to set clearer goals for your future. Ask yourself: does your current path align with your values and passions? If not, today offers clarity about adjustments that could move you closer to authenticity. Don't dismiss small steps—they often lead to major breakthroughs over time. Trust that your unique gifts are ready to be shared more fully with the world.

Affirmation & Gratitude

I align my ambitions with purpose, taking confident steps toward success.

Pisces
20 June 2026

Pisces, today the cosmos encourages rest and introspection. You may feel quieter, craving solitude to restore your energy. Don't resist this pull—honor it. Dreams or intuitive nudges may be particularly vivid, offering subtle yet powerful guidance. Spend time journaling, meditating, or simply allowing your mind to wander. This is not withdrawal—it's a conscious choice to reconnect with yourself. Reflection today prepares you for clarity and renewed energy in the coming days.

Affirmation & Gratitude

I honor rest as essential, knowing stillness brings clarity and strength.

Pisces
21 June 2026

Pisces, the Solstice and Sun's shift into Cancer brings warmth to your creative and romantic sector. Over the weeks ahead, you'll be inspired to express yourself more freely and to nurture joy. Today, you may already feel sparks of inspiration—whether in art, hobbies, or matters of the heart. Creativity flows more easily when you allow yourself to play without judgment. Romance is also highlighted—connections feel deeper and more heartfelt under this solstice light.

Affirmation & Gratitude

I embrace joy and creativity, allowing inspiration and love to flow through me.

Pisces
22 June 2026

Pisces, today's energy emphasizes responsibility and structure. You may feel called to focus on health, routines, or practical tasks. While not glamorous, these steps create a solid base for your bigger dreams. Don't let overwhelm stop you—take things one step at a time. Small adjustments now will have lasting benefits. Balance responsibility with compassion for yourself, and you'll find progress feels steady rather than draining.

Affirmation & Gratitude

I create stability through small, steady steps that honor my wellbeing.

Pisces
23 June 2026

Pisces, relationships come into focus today. Emotional conversations may arise, giving you a chance to deepen connections or clear misunderstandings. Be open, but also protect your boundaries—balance is essential. Your compassion allows others to feel safe sharing, but remember to honor your own needs. If single, today may bring insights about what you truly seek in partnership. Authentic connection grows when you're honest with yourself first.

Affirmation & Gratitude

I welcome authentic connections, honoring both my heart and my boundaries.

Pisces
24 June 2026

Pisces, today's Full Moon in Capricorn lights up your community and friendship sector. You may realize which connections support your growth and which feel draining. A group project may come to a climax, bringing clarity about next steps. While emotions may run high, this lunation offers closure and the chance to realign your social circle with your values. Celebrate the friendships that uplift you, and gracefully release those that no longer resonate.

Affirmation & Gratitude

I honor friendships that inspire me, releasing those that no longer align.

Pisces
25 June 2026

Pisces, the energy today feels lighter after yesterday's Full Moon. You may sense a release, as though something has shifted in your social or community connections. Take time to integrate what you've learned about boundaries and belonging. Reflect on who truly supports your growth and who drains your spirit. Spend time with uplifting people and allow yourself to step away from those who no longer align. Trust that letting go makes space for deeper, more authentic connections.

Affirmation & Gratitude

I choose community that uplifts and honors my spirit, releasing what no longer serves.

Pisces
26 June 2026

Pisces, today your focus may turn inward as you reflect on recent changes. Emotional clarity comes through stillness, so give yourself time for journaling, meditation, or simply sitting quietly with your thoughts. You may uncover insights about what you need to feel more secure and fulfilled. Don't be afraid to face truths—they are guideposts, not obstacles. By acknowledging what lies beneath the surface, you open yourself to healing and alignment.

Affirmation & Gratitude

I honor reflection, trusting inner truths to guide me toward healing and clarity.

Pisces
27 June 2026

Pisces, today the cosmos emphasizes expansion and learning. You may feel drawn toward new ideas, travel, or spiritual exploration. Inspiration flows when you step beyond the familiar. A book, conversation, or new experience could spark fresh insight and shift your perspective. Don't resist the urge to broaden your world—growth thrives when you're willing to take risks. Today is about opening your heart and mind to possibility.

Affirmation & Gratitude

I embrace exploration with curiosity, welcoming wisdom in new forms.

Pisces
28 June 2026

Pisces, career matters may come to the forefront today. Recognition for past efforts may arrive, or you may feel motivated to pursue a new direction that better reflects your values. If you've been questioning your path, clarity begins to emerge. Take practical steps toward long-term goals, even if small. Remember, steady progress is more sustainable than sudden leaps. Align your ambitions with authenticity and trust that success will follow.

Affirmation & Gratitude

I align my work with my truth, trusting each step builds a meaningful future.

Pisces
29 June 2026

Pisces, today's energy highlights rest and introspection. You may feel more sensitive than usual, craving solitude. Don't push yourself—honor the need for quiet. Dreams may carry important guidance, so pay attention to the messages that surface in sleep or meditation. This is a day for gentle self-care and spiritual practices. Restoring your energy now will prepare you for what's ahead.

Affirmation & Gratitude

I honor rest as sacred, trusting renewal strengthens my spirit.

Pisces
30 June 2026

Pisces, transformation is highlighted today. Emotional intensity may arise, but it signals where change is needed. Whether it's releasing old patterns, shifting beliefs, or ending cycles, trust that letting go is part of growth. While it may feel uncomfortable, it opens space for new beginnings. A powerful realization may help you see where freedom lies. Embrace the process—transformation is not loss, but liberation.

Affirmation & Gratitude

I release with courage, welcoming transformation as a path to freedom.

July
2026

Pisces
01 July 2026

Pisces, the new month begins with fresh inspiration and focus. You may feel energized to pursue goals, refine plans, or step into new opportunities. The cosmos encourages clarity—set intentions for July with both practicality and vision. Choose one or two priorities rather than scattering your energy. You'll find progress flows more easily when you direct your efforts with purpose. Trust that momentum is building in your favor.

Affirmation & Gratitude

I set clear intentions, aligning focus with purpose for the month ahead.

Pisces
02 July 2026

Pisces, today the cosmos highlights communication. You may feel inspired to share your ideas or have meaningful conversations that bring clarity. Writing, teaching, or journaling can also be powerful tools for self-expression. Be mindful of your words—they hold extra influence now. If misunderstandings have lingered, this is the day to clear the air with honesty and compassion. The universe reminds you that your voice is a gift—use it to uplift, not diminish.

Affirmation & Gratitude

I express myself with honesty and compassion, knowing my words carry healing power.

Pisces
03 July 2026

Pisces, your home and family sector feels emphasized today. You may crave comfort and stability, whether through time with loved ones or by tending to your personal space. Emotional matters may arise, offering a chance for resolution and deeper understanding. Creating peace at home sets the tone for everything else in your life. Even small acts of care—like tidying, cooking, or spending time together—bring grounding and harmony.

Affirmation & Gratitude

I create harmony in my home and heart, honoring the peace I need.

Pisces
04 July 2026

Pisces, today's energy invites expansion and exploration. You may feel called to learn, travel, or immerse yourself in new ideas. Inspiration could come through a mentor, a class, or even a conversation that shifts your outlook. The cosmos encourages you to embrace curiosity—it will guide you toward growth. Don't hold back from stepping beyond your comfort zone. Even small explorations today can ripple into long-term wisdom and opportunity.

Affirmation & Gratitude

I welcome growth and new perspectives with an open and curious spirit.

Pisces
05 July 2026

Pisces, today the focus shifts toward career and purpose. Recognition for your work may arrive, or you may feel called to take action toward your long-term goals. Ask yourself if your current path feels aligned with your soul. If adjustments are needed, clarity will come through reflection and practical planning. Take a step, however small, toward what feels authentic. The universe supports ambition when it's fueled by truth.

Affirmation & Gratitude

I align my ambitions with authenticity, trusting each step shapes my purpose.

Pisces
06 July 2026

Pisces, today invites quiet reflection. Your energy may feel softer, and you could crave solitude or spiritual practices that restore balance. Pay attention to your dreams or intuitive nudges—they may carry important guidance. Avoid forcing productivity; instead, allow rest to recharge your spirit. Today's stillness is fertile ground for insights that will guide you in the weeks ahead.

Affirmation & Gratitude

I embrace rest and reflection, trusting stillness to bring clarity.

Pisces
07 July 2026

Pisces, transformation energy surrounds you today. Old fears, patterns, or beliefs may resurface, asking to be released once and for all. While the process may feel emotional, it's also profoundly healing. Lean into honesty with yourself—acknowledge what you've outgrown and step forward without regret. Transformation doesn't mean losing yourself; it means shedding what no longer serves your highest potential. Trust the process of renewal.

Affirmation & Gratitude

I release the past with courage, welcoming transformation as growth.

Pisces
08 July 2026

Pisces, today's cosmic energy highlights friendships and community. You may feel more social, drawn to connect with like-minded people who inspire you. Group activities or collaborations may spark creativity and joy. Pay attention to how your energy feels in different circles—choose to invest in the connections that uplift you. Your spirit thrives when surrounded by community that honors your authentic self. Celebrate shared purpose and joy.

Affirmation & Gratitude

I welcome community that uplifts and inspires me, honoring authentic connection.

Pisces
09 July 2026

Pisces, today's energy encourages rest and introspection. You may feel quieter, needing time to process recent events or emotions. Don't force yourself into busyness—reflection is valuable in its own right. Dreams and intuition may feel heightened, offering insights into your next steps. Gentle activities like journaling, meditation, or spending time in nature will be especially nourishing. Allow yourself to retreat, knowing that stillness often reveals truths that action alone cannot.

Affirmation & Gratitude

I honor rest and reflection, trusting wisdom rises in stillness.

Pisces
10 July 2026

Pisces, today's cosmic energy highlights expansion and learning. You may feel drawn to study, travel, or explore new ideas that excite your spirit. Even small explorations—like reading something different or connecting with someone outside your usual circle—can spark inspiration. Growth comes from openness, and the universe is nudging you toward experiences that broaden your horizons. Follow curiosity—it's your compass for the day.

Affirmation & Gratitude

I embrace curiosity and welcome wisdom in every form it arrives.

Pisces
11 July 2026

Pisces, your career and ambitions may take center stage today. Recognition for your past efforts could arrive, or you may feel motivated to step into new responsibility. Ask yourself: does your current path reflect your values? If not, today provides clarity and the chance to pivot. Even small changes made now will ripple into meaningful progress later. Align your ambition with authenticity, and success will follow naturally.

Affirmation & Gratitude

I pursue goals that honor my truth, trusting success flows from authenticity.

Pisces
12 July 2026

Pisces, today emphasizes introspection and spiritual connection. You may feel the need to withdraw from external demands and spend time nurturing your inner world. Pay attention to intuitive nudges, dreams, or synchronicities—they're carrying guidance. Don't dismiss subtle whispers; they may contain exactly the insight you need. This is a powerful day for meditation, creative flow, and spiritual practices that restore your soul.

Affirmation & Gratitude

I listen to my intuition and trust the quiet wisdom it offers me.

Pisces
13 July 2026

Pisces, today brings transformation energy to the forefront. Emotional intensity may surface, revealing what you're ready to release. While this process may feel heavy, it is necessary for growth. Old fears or habits may resurface, not to haunt you but to remind you of how far you've come. Release with love and gratitude, knowing each ending makes space for renewal. Transformation is your ally, guiding you toward authenticity.

Affirmation & Gratitude

I release the old with gratitude, embracing transformation as my path to freedom.

Pisces
14 July 2026

Pisces, friendships and community take the spotlight today. You may feel called to connect with those who inspire and uplift you. Group activities may spark joy and remind you of the importance of shared vision. At the same time, notice where your energy feels drained—it may be time to set firmer boundaries. Surround yourself with community that celebrates your authenticity. The right connections bring confidence and joy.

Affirmation & Gratitude

I welcome friendships that uplift my spirit and honor my true self.

Pisces
15 July 2026

Pisces, today's energy turns inward again, encouraging rest and reflection. Solitude may feel more appealing than socializing. Give yourself time to recharge, especially if you've been emotionally stretched. Pay attention to dreams or intuitive whispers; they may reveal guidance for the days ahead. This is not withdrawal—it's intentional restoration. Trust that you're gathering strength for the next chapter.

Affirmation & Gratitude

I embrace solitude with love, trusting it restores my spirit and clarity.

Pisces
16 July 2026

Pisces, today's energy invites expansion and growth. You may feel a surge of curiosity or the desire to step beyond your comfort zone. This could involve learning, travel, or simply exploring a new idea that sparks excitement. The universe encourages you to remain open to opportunities that broaden your perspective. Conversations with mentors or friends may hold valuable insights. Growth often comes from saying yes to what feels unfamiliar.

Affirmation & Gratitude

I embrace new experiences and allow curiosity to guide me into growth.

Pisces
17 July 2026

Pisces, career and recognition come into focus today. Your efforts may be acknowledged, or you could feel motivated to take a bold step toward your goals. The universe reminds you that steady effort creates lasting results. If doubts surface, remember your unique gifts are worthy of being shared. Align ambition with authenticity, and you'll attract opportunities that match your soul's truth. Practical action today supports your long-term vision.

Affirmation & Gratitude

I take confident steps toward goals that honor my true purpose.

Pisces
18 July 2026

Pisces, the cosmos encourages introspection today. You may crave quiet, sensing that answers lie within rather than in external validation. Allow yourself to slow down and tune into your inner voice. Spiritual practices feel especially powerful—dream journaling, meditation, or prayer may bring clarity. Don't underestimate the wisdom of silence; it's often where your deepest truths emerge. Trust your intuition, even if it contradicts logic.

Affirmation & Gratitude

I honor silence and reflection, trusting my intuition to guide me.

Pisces
19 July 2026

Pisces, transformation energy surrounds you today. Emotions may rise strongly, reminding you of what's ready to be released. Whether it's a fear, a pattern, or a relationship dynamic, trust that letting go will free you. Transformation can feel like loss, but it's actually an opening. Lean into the process with courage and compassion for yourself. Remember that you are evolving into alignment with your authentic self.

Affirmation & Gratitude

I release the old with courage, trusting transformation as my ally.

Pisces
20 July 2026

Pisces, friendships and community are emphasized today. You may feel drawn to gather with like-minded souls, collaborate, or simply enjoy meaningful connections. Surround yourself with those who inspire and uplift you—these relationships fuel your spirit. At the same time, pay attention to where you feel drained; boundaries may need to be set. Celebrate the joy of belonging while maintaining your individuality.

Affirmation & Gratitude

I cherish connections that uplift me and celebrate authentic community.

Pisces
21 July 2026

Pisces, today's energy invites rest and reflection. After recent social or emotional activity, your spirit needs solitude to reset. Don't see this as isolation—it's a chance to restore your energy and listen inward. Pay attention to your dreams; they may hold messages about your next steps. Quiet time will help you integrate recent lessons and prepare for what's ahead.

Affirmation & Gratitude

I embrace solitude as healing, knowing it restores my clarity and strength.

Pisces
22 July 2026

Pisces, the Sun shifts into Leo today, shining light on your daily routines, health, and responsibilities. Over the coming weeks, you'll be encouraged to create more structure and balance in your everyday life. Today, you may feel the first nudge to review habits and routines. Ask yourself if they support your energy or drain it. The cosmos reminds you that small, consistent changes bring long-term vitality and flow.

Affirmation & Gratitude

I create supportive routines that honor my body, mind, and spirit.

Pisces
23 July 2026

Pisces, today's cosmic energy highlights your daily routines and responsibilities. You may feel nudged to bring more structure into your life, whether through organization, health practices, or time management. Though routine isn't always your favorite, the stars remind you that it creates freedom in the long run. Even small shifts—like a healthier meal or a clearer schedule—can have lasting benefits. Focus on progress, not perfection. Each step you take today strengthens the foundation for your bigger dreams.

Affirmation & Gratitude

I honor small steps that create balance and stability in my daily life.

Pisces
24 July 2026

Pisces, relationships take center stage today. You may feel called to connect more deeply with a partner, friend, or colleague. Honest conversations open doors for healing and growth. At the same time, notice where balance may be off—are you giving more than you receive? Boundaries don't block love; they protect it. Today is a reminder that healthy connections flourish when both sides feel seen and valued.

Affirmation & Gratitude

I welcome relationships that honor balance, respect, and mutual care.

Pisces
25 July 2026

Pisces, today's energy highlights your health and wellbeing. You may feel motivated to improve daily habits that support your body and spirit. Exercise, nourishing food, or mindful rest will have extra impact now. Don't pressure yourself into drastic change —gentle consistency is more sustainable. If your schedule has been chaotic, today offers clarity about where adjustments can restore balance. Your body speaks; listen closely to what it needs.

Affirmation & Gratitude

I care for my body with love, creating harmony through steady habits.

Pisces
26 July 2026

Pisces, curiosity and growth are emphasized today. You may feel inspired to explore new ideas, cultures, or philosophies. Conversations with others could spark insights, or you may find wisdom in unexpected places. The universe is urging you to keep your mind open. Even small steps toward learning can expand your perspective and open doors to new opportunities. Curiosity today is a seed for future growth.

Affirmation & Gratitude

I welcome learning and exploration, allowing curiosity to expand my world.

Pisces
27 July 2026

Pisces, career and long-term goals are in the spotlight today. Recognition may come your way, or you may feel more determined to pursue your ambitions. Ask yourself whether your current path reflects your authentic self. If not, consider small adjustments that move you closer to alignment. Remember, ambition doesn't have to be forceful—your quiet determination carries strength. Trust that each step brings you closer to lasting success.

Affirmation & Gratitude

I align my ambitions with authenticity, moving steadily toward success.

Pisces
28 July 2026

Pisces, today encourages rest and inner reflection. You may feel more sensitive than usual, needing quiet space to recharge. Solitude is not weakness—it's nourishment. Pay attention to dreams or inner whispers, as they may guide you toward clarity. Avoid overwhelming yourself with external demands; instead, honor your inner rhythm. By slowing down, you'll find inspiration and renewal waiting for you.

Affirmation & Gratitude

I honor solitude and rest, trusting stillness to restore my strength.

Pisces
29 July 2026

Pisces, transformation energy flows strongly today. Old fears, beliefs, or habits may resurface, asking to be released. While this may feel emotional, it is also deeply freeing. Trust that the universe is guiding you to shed what no longer serves your highest good. Release with compassion—growth doesn't come from holding on, but from letting go. Transformation today may be subtle yet powerful, shaping your future with greater authenticity.

Affirmation & Gratitude

I release with courage, opening space for renewal and alignment.

Pisces
30 July 2026

Pisces, today's energy draws your attention to friendships and community. You may feel uplifted by the company of those who share your values and dreams. Collaboration can spark inspiration, and a group project could move forward successfully. At the same time, pay attention to where you feel drained—boundaries may need to be strengthened. The cosmos is asking you to align with people who celebrate your authenticity. Collective energy can be a powerful force when it's rooted in love and mutual respect.

Affirmation & Gratitude

I cherish connections that inspire me and honor the joy of authentic community.

Pisces
31 July 2026

Pisces, introspection takes center stage today. You may crave quiet time away from the noise of daily life. This is a good day for meditation, journaling, or simply resting in solitude. Pay attention to your dreams or intuitive nudges—they may be showing you the next step in your journey. Don't force productivity; your inner world holds the guidance you need. By honoring reflection, you create space for clarity to arise naturally.

Affirmation & Gratitude

I embrace solitude as sacred, allowing wisdom to flow through silence.

August 2026

Pisces
01 August 2026

Pisces, a new month begins with transformative energy. The cosmos highlights release and renewal—you may feel ready to let go of a burden you've carried for too long. This could be an old fear, limiting belief, or emotional attachment. Though letting go may feel bittersweet, trust that it is creating space for new beginnings. Transformation today empowers you to step into greater authenticity and freedom. Remember, endings always carry the seeds of fresh starts.

Affirmation & Gratitude

I release with gratitude, trusting transformation to guide me into freedom.

Pisces
02 August 2026

Pisces, today's energy emphasizes friendships and networks. You may find yourself surrounded by people who inspire and uplift you, reminding you of the power of shared purpose. Collaboration may feel especially rewarding now. At the same time, you might notice certain connections no longer resonate—don't be afraid to adjust where you invest your energy. Your spirit thrives in circles that celebrate your authenticity.

Affirmation & Gratitude

I align with friendships that nourish my soul and uplift my spirit.

Pisces
03 August 2026

Pisces, today brings rest and reflection. You may feel a pull to slow down and listen to your inner world. Allow yourself time for quiet, whether through meditation, journaling, or simply being in nature. Dreams or intuitive whispers may be especially vivid, offering subtle guidance. Don't see stillness as inactivity—it's the preparation ground for future action. Today is about nurturing your spirit and allowing wisdom to surface naturally.

Affirmation & Gratitude

I honor stillness, knowing reflection brings clarity and renewal.

Pisces
04 August 2026

Pisces, transformation energy continues today. You may feel emotions surfacing, showing you what's ready to be released. While this may be uncomfortable, it is also liberating. The universe is helping you shed what no longer serves your growth, creating room for new opportunities. Lean into the process with compassion for yourself. Trust that by letting go, you are aligning with your highest potential.

Affirmation & Gratitude

I let go with love, trusting transformation to lead me to freedom.

Pisces
05 August 2026

Pisces, today's cosmic energy highlights expansion and learning. You may feel inspired to explore new ideas, engage in study, or seek experiences that broaden your perspective. Inspiration can arrive through a teacher, mentor, or even a chance encounter. The universe is encouraging you to open your mind to wisdom in all forms. Curiosity is your guide—follow it and allow it to lead you toward growth and deeper understanding.

Affirmation & Gratitude

I welcome wisdom in every form, trusting curiosity to expand my horizons.

Pisces
06 August 2026

Pisces, your career and ambitions take the spotlight today. You may feel recognition for your efforts, or clarity may emerge about the next step you want to take. The universe encourages you to align ambition with authenticity—success feels hollow if it doesn't reflect your soul's truth. Practical planning will be especially helpful now. A small step today could ripple into long-term achievement. Trust your talents; they are ready to shine more fully.

Affirmation & Gratitude

I align my ambitions with authenticity, trusting my work to reflect my soul's truth.

Pisces
07 August 2026

Pisces, today invites you to rest and restore. After recent focus on outer responsibilities, your spirit craves inner nourishment. Spend time in quiet reflection, whether through journaling, meditation, or simply being in nature. This is a day to release pressure and allow peace to fill the spaces where stress has been. Pay attention to dreams or subtle nudges from the universe—they carry messages meant for you.

Affirmation & Gratitude

I honor rest and stillness, trusting renewal strengthens my spirit.

Pisces
08 August 2026

Pisces, today transformation is emphasized. Old fears, beliefs, or attachments may surface, asking for acknowledgment and release. Though it may feel uncomfortable, this is an opportunity for profound healing. The cosmos reminds you that letting go isn't about loss but about creating space for growth. Trust that the universe is preparing you for something greater. Lean into the process with courage and compassion—you are stronger than you realize.

Affirmation & Gratitude

I release what no longer serves me, welcoming transformation as growth.

Pisces
09 August 2026

Pisces, today friendships and community are highlighted. You may feel inspired to connect with like-minded people or join a group that shares your values. Collaboration can spark joy and creativity, while uplifting conversations remind you of the importance of shared vision. Notice which connections nourish your spirit and which drain it. Align yourself with people who support your growth and authenticity.

Affirmation & Gratitude

I value friendships that inspire me and celebrate authentic connection.

Pisces
10 August 2026

Pisces, today's energy turns inward. You may feel quieter, drawn to solitude or spiritual practices. Don't dismiss this pull—it's a chance to restore balance and clarity. Pay attention to intuition and dreams; they may reveal insights about decisions or next steps. Rest is productive now, helping you align with the flow of life. Trust the wisdom that comes in stillness.

Affirmation & Gratitude

I embrace solitude as sacred, trusting it restores my clarity and strength.

Pisces
11 August 2026

Pisces, today emphasizes curiosity and expansion. You may feel the desire to learn, travel, or explore fresh perspectives. Even a small step—like trying something new or having a meaningful conversation—can spark inspiration. The cosmos reminds you that growth is continuous, and openness is your greatest tool. Don't hesitate to follow the paths that excite your heart.

Affirmation & Gratitude

I welcome new experiences with openness, trusting they lead me toward growth.

Pisces
12 August 2026

Pisces, your career and sense of purpose come into focus again. Recognition may arrive, or you may feel motivated to set clearer long-term goals. Don't shy away from responsibility—your quiet persistence carries strength others notice. Aligning your work with your values ensures success feels fulfilling. A small action today—sending an email, updating plans, or making a commitment—can set powerful energy in motion.

Affirmation & Gratitude

I take purposeful steps toward success, aligning ambition with authenticity.

Pisces
13 August 2026

Pisces, today the cosmos encourages reflection and inner renewal. You may feel drawn to step away from external noise and focus on your inner voice. Spiritual practices are deeply supportive now—journaling, meditation, or simply resting in stillness will help you recharge. Emotions may surface unexpectedly, but don't judge them; they're guiding you to clarity. Sometimes the answers you seek don't arrive through action but through quiet awareness. Let yourself listen without forcing outcomes.

Affirmation & Gratitude

I honor stillness and reflection, trusting inner wisdom to guide me.

Pisces
14 August 2026

Pisces, today transformation is highlighted. Old fears, patterns, or habits may rise to the surface, asking to be acknowledged and released. Though this may feel uncomfortable, it is also empowering. The universe is helping you shed what no longer serves your growth. Trust that each release makes space for renewal. Lean into honesty with yourself and allow change to unfold naturally. Liberation comes when you stop holding onto what keeps you small.

Affirmation & Gratitude

I release with courage, embracing transformation as a step into freedom.

Pisces
15 August 2026

Pisces, today highlights friendships and social connections. You may feel inspired to spend time with people who uplift you or to seek out new communities aligned with your values. Collaboration can bring unexpected inspiration. At the same time, notice where you feel drained—it may be time to step back from certain dynamics. Authentic community supports your growth, while shallow ties only weigh you down. Choose your connections wisely.

Affirmation & Gratitude

I cherish friendships that inspire me and align with my authentic self.

Pisces
16 August 2026

Pisces, introspection takes priority today. You may crave quiet or feel the need to retreat into your inner world. This is a good day to process recent changes and reconnect with your intuition. Dreams may be vivid, carrying messages from your subconscious. Pay attention to subtle signs—they're pointing you toward alignment. Avoid overwhelming yourself with obligations; solitude and self-care will help restore clarity and peace.

Affirmation & Gratitude

I embrace solitude as healing, allowing clarity to rise within me.

Pisces
17 August 2026

Pisces, today's energy is expansive, urging you to explore new perspectives. Learning, travel, or deep conversations could spark inspiration. Even small shifts—like reading something outside your usual interests—can open doors. The universe is asking you to remain open to fresh ideas that broaden your vision. Growth happens when you stretch beyond the familiar, so don't hesitate to follow curiosity. It may lead you exactly where you need to go.

Affirmation & Gratitude

I welcome new perspectives, trusting growth comes from openness.

Pisces
18 August 2026

Pisces, career and purpose are in focus today. Recognition for your work may come, or you may feel inspired to take a more defined step toward your ambitions. Align your goals with what feels authentic—true success is rooted in integrity. A mentor or colleague may offer encouragement or guidance. This is a day to believe in your abilities and take practical action that supports your long-term vision.

Affirmation & Gratitude

I align my ambitions with authenticity, trusting each step builds success.

Pisces
19 August 2026

Pisces, today's energy turns inward again, reminding you to nurture your spirit. You may feel more sensitive, and solitude will be healing. Pay attention to dreams, signs, or intuitive whispers—they may reveal insights about your next steps. This is not a day for rushing; it's a day for listening. Trust that reflection now will prepare you for clarity and action soon. Be gentle with yourself as you honor your inner rhythm.

Affirmation & Gratitude

I honor my inner rhythm, trusting reflection as a guide to clarity.

Pisces
20 August 2026

Pisces, today the cosmos emphasizes transformation once again. Old patterns or attachments may resurface, asking you to reflect on whether they still belong in your life. While facing these truths can feel heavy, the universe is guiding you toward release and renewal. Transformation is rarely comfortable, but it is always liberating. Allow yourself to grieve what is leaving while celebrating the space being created for something better. Trust this process—it is shaping your path toward authenticity.

Affirmation & Gratitude

I release with trust, knowing transformation clears space for brighter beginnings.

Pisces
21 August 2026

Pisces, friendships and community are highlighted today. You may feel uplifted by conversations or inspired by the company of like-minded souls. Collaboration is favored—working with others could spark ideas and joy. Pay attention to the energy exchanges within your connections. If you notice imbalance, it may be time to adjust. Celebrate the relationships that nourish you, and gracefully distance yourself from those that deplete your spirit.

Affirmation & Gratitude

I value uplifting connections and align with friendships that honor my energy.

Pisces
22 August 2026

Pisces, today's energy encourages rest and reflection. You may crave solitude, needing time to integrate recent lessons. Don't push yourself into social activity if your spirit needs quiet. Dreams may be especially vivid, carrying guidance for your next steps. Journaling or meditation could reveal insights. Stillness is not wasted time—it's where wisdom blooms. Allow yourself to retreat into the sanctuary of your inner world.

Affirmation & Gratitude

I embrace solitude and reflection, trusting my spirit to find renewal in stillness.

Pisces
23 August 2026

Pisces, today the Sun moves into Virgo, illuminating your relationship sector. Over the coming weeks, partnerships—both romantic and professional—will take priority. Today, you may already feel shifts in how you relate to others. Balance, clarity, and mutual respect are key themes. The universe is encouraging you to evaluate your connections honestly and nurture those that feel aligned. Harmony grows when both sides feel seen and supported.

Affirmation & Gratitude

I welcome balanced partnerships built on honesty, respect, and care.

Pisces
24 August 2026

Pisces, your daily routines and wellbeing are emphasized today. You may feel inspired to bring more order to your schedule or focus on health habits that strengthen your body and mind. Even small steps, like organizing your day or nourishing your body, create ripple effects. Don't let perfectionism stop you—progress is more important than flawless execution. Consistency is your ally now.

Affirmation & Gratitude

I honor my wellbeing by creating small, steady habits that bring harmony.

Pisces
25 August 2026

Pisces, today brings opportunities for learning and exploration. You may feel drawn to study, travel, or open your mind to new philosophies. Curiosity is your compass, and following it can lead to valuable insights. Conversations with others may inspire you, or a new experience could shift your perspective in powerful ways. Growth is waiting, but you must say yes to it. Let curiosity guide you into fresh territory.

Affirmation & Gratitude

I embrace curiosity and welcome wisdom in all its forms.

Pisces
26 August 2026

Pisces, your career and purpose take the spotlight today. Recognition for your hard work could arrive, or clarity about your next steps may emerge. Don't dismiss small opportunities—they could open doors to something bigger. Align your ambitions with authenticity, and you'll feel more fulfilled in your progress. Trust your talents and share them with confidence. The universe supports you when you commit to your path with integrity.

Affirmation & Gratitude

I take confident steps toward my purpose, aligning ambition with authenticity.

Pisces
27 August 2026

Pisces, today invites you to slow down and listen to your inner voice. You may feel more sensitive than usual, noticing subtle emotional shifts within yourself or others. Rather than pushing ahead, embrace stillness. Journaling or meditation can reveal truths you've been overlooking. This is a good day to nurture your emotional health, as clarity will follow. By honoring your inner world, you create balance that strengthens your outer one. Don't underestimate the power of quiet reflection—it's transformative.

Affirmation & Gratitude

I honor my emotions and trust the wisdom that surfaces in stillness.

Pisces
28 August 2026

Pisces, transformation energy continues to surround you today. The cosmos is asking you to let go of lingering doubts, fears, or attachments. This process may feel emotional, but it will leave you feeling lighter and freer. Pay attention to areas where you've been resisting change—these are where breakthroughs are waiting. Allow yourself to release gently, without judgment. The more you surrender, the easier the path becomes. Trust that letting go is leading you toward greater alignment.

Affirmation & Gratitude

I release with compassion, trusting transformation to open new doors.

Pisces
29 August 2026

Pisces, today highlights friendships and social connections. You may feel called to spend time with people who inspire and uplift you, or you could reconnect with someone from your past who reminds you of your growth. Collaboration may bring progress, and networking can open unexpected opportunities. Be mindful of energy exchanges—choose to invest in relationships that nourish your soul. Celebrate community while remembering the importance of your individuality.

Affirmation & Gratitude

I align with friendships that honor my authenticity and inspire joy.

Pisces
30 August 2026

Pisces, today's energy turns inward. You may feel the need to retreat and reflect, allowing your body and mind to rest. Dreams and intuition may be particularly vivid now, offering subtle but powerful guidance. Solitude doesn't mean loneliness —it's a chance to recharge and reconnect with your inner self. Don't pressure yourself into productivity; restoration is your priority today. Trust that clarity and strength will return once you've honored this pause.

Affirmation & Gratitude

I embrace rest as sacred, allowing solitude to renew my spirit.

Pisces
31 August 2026

Pisces, curiosity and exploration are encouraged today. You may feel pulled toward new learning, travel, or philosophical insights. Inspiration might arrive in a conversation, a book, or even a chance encounter. Allow yourself to be guided by wonder and openness. Sometimes, the smallest experiences lead to the biggest shifts in perspective. The universe is reminding you that wisdom is everywhere—you only need to stay receptive to it.

Affirmation & Gratitude

I welcome new perspectives with an open heart and mind.

September 2026

Pisces
01 September 2026

Pisces, career and purpose are emphasized today. Recognition may arrive for your hard work, or you may feel clearer about what direction you want to pursue. If doubts arise, ask yourself whether your goals align with your deeper values. When your ambitions reflect your true self, success feels meaningful. Practical steps today—however small—set the foundation for greater progress. Trust that your dedication is moving you closer to fulfillment.

Affirmation & Gratitude

I pursue goals that honor my truth, trusting success flows from authenticity.

Pisces
02 September 2026

Pisces, today encourages reflection and inner renewal. You may feel more sensitive, noticing subtle signs from your intuition or through dreams. Don't dismiss these messages—they're guiding you toward alignment. This is an excellent day for spiritual practices, meditation, or journaling. Avoid external distractions where possible; your energy is best spent listening inward. Stillness brings the clarity you've been seeking. Trust the whispers of your soul—they're speaking loudly today.

Affirmation & Gratitude

I trust my intuition, knowing it leads me toward clarity and peace.

Pisces
03 September 2026

Pisces, today transformation energy rises again, asking you to face what you've been avoiding. Old fears, habits, or even unresolved emotions could resurface, not to unsettle you but to guide you toward release. The cosmos reminds you that you cannot carry everything forward—something must be let go to make room for growth. Although the process feels intense, liberation is waiting on the other side. Be gentle with yourself and honor your emotions as they flow.

Affirmation & Gratitude

I release with compassion, trusting transformation clears space for freedom and growth.

Pisces
04 September 2026

Pisces, friendships and community connections feel highlighted today. You may notice which relationships truly support your spirit and which ones weigh you down. The stars encourage you to invest in uplifting circles while gently stepping back from those that drain your energy. Collaboration and teamwork can thrive under today's energy, provided everyone shares the same vision. Celebrate the joy of authentic belonging and allow yourself to shine within your community.

Affirmation & Gratitude

I choose friendships that inspire joy and align with my authenticity.

Pisces
05 September 2026

Pisces, today invites introspection and rest. You may crave solitude, feeling that your energy is better spent within than without. This is a day for reflection, meditation, or simply allowing your spirit to recharge. Dreams may carry guidance, so pay attention to subtle details. Don't feel guilty for stepping back—the stillness is restoring your strength. Sometimes, doing less creates space for clarity and renewal.

Affirmation & Gratitude

I honor rest as essential, trusting stillness restores my spirit.

Pisces
06 September 2026

Pisces, today's energy emphasizes curiosity and exploration. You may feel called to learn, study, or engage in conversations that expand your perspective. The universe is urging you to open your mind to new insights. Even a small step, like diving into a new subject, can lead to breakthroughs. Don't shy away from fresh opportunities—they could reveal paths you hadn't considered before. Follow your curiosity with openness.

Affirmation & Gratitude

I welcome new learning and allow curiosity to guide me forward.

Pisces
07 September 2026

Pisces, your career and long-term goals are emphasized today. Recognition for your hard work could arrive, or clarity about your ambitions may become more defined. The stars encourage you to take practical steps toward your purpose. Aligning ambition with authenticity ensures your progress feels fulfilling, not forced. Be mindful of opportunities that align with your truth, and don't fear stepping into responsibility—you are capable of much more than you think.

Affirmation & Gratitude

I take confident steps toward success, aligning ambition with authenticity.

Pisces
08 September 2026

Pisces, today invites reflection and solitude. You may feel sensitive, picking up on the energies of others more strongly than usual. Protect your energy and retreat when necessary. This is a day to tune into your inner world—dreams, journaling, or meditation will reveal guidance. Avoid overextending yourself socially or professionally; self-care is essential now. Honor your boundaries and trust that renewal is part of your path.

Affirmation & Gratitude

I protect my energy and honor solitude as part of my healing.

Pisces
09 September 2026

Pisces, today's cosmic energy encourages transformation and release. Emotions may surface strongly, but they are guiding you to what is ready to end. Whether it's a habit, relationship pattern, or limiting thought, trust that releasing it creates space for freedom. Change may feel daunting, but you are ready. Transformation clears old weight and brings fresh perspective. Allow yourself to surrender with love—it's the doorway to a lighter future.

Affirmation & Gratitude

I release with love, trusting transformation guides me into freedom.

Pisces
10 September 2026

Pisces, today highlights friendships and community. You may feel inspired to reconnect with people who share your passions or to join a new circle that uplifts you. Group efforts are favored, and collaboration can spark powerful ideas. Be mindful of where your energy feels nourished and where it feels drained. Authentic connections will energize you, while shallow ties may feel heavy. The stars remind you to honor the difference and invest in what feels true.

Affirmation & Gratitude

I align with friendships that inspire me and honor my authentic spirit.

Pisces
11 September 2026

Pisces, today the cosmos encourages reflection and stillness. You may feel more sensitive than usual, picking up on subtle energies around you. This is a day for solitude, self-care, and spiritual practice. Journaling or meditation may reveal insights that help you understand recent experiences more clearly. Don't pressure yourself to achieve; instead, allow yourself to recharge. Renewal happens when you create space for your inner voice to be heard.

Affirmation & Gratitude

I honor quiet moments, trusting reflection to restore my balance and clarity.

Pisces
12 September 2026

Pisces, transformation is in focus today. You may be asked to release what no longer aligns with your higher path. This could be an outdated habit, fear, or relationship pattern. While it may feel challenging, it's also liberating. Change clears space for growth and helps you step into greater authenticity. Trust that what leaves your life now is making room for something more aligned with your soul's purpose.

Affirmation & Gratitude

I release with courage, welcoming transformation as a step into freedom.

Pisces
13 September 2026

Pisces, today's energy emphasizes exploration and expansion. You may feel drawn to study, travel, or connect with people who broaden your perspective. The stars encourage you to remain curious—every conversation or experience could hold valuable wisdom. Allow yourself to step outside your comfort zone. Even a small act of openness today could ripple into long-term inspiration and growth. Follow the nudges—they're leading you toward wisdom.

Affirmation & Gratitude

I embrace curiosity and welcome new experiences as pathways to growth.

Pisces
14 September 2026

Pisces, career and recognition are highlighted today. Your efforts may be acknowledged, or you may feel motivated to set clearer goals. Align your ambitions with your authentic self for lasting fulfillment. Practical steps taken today could yield progress that lasts. Don't shy away from responsibility—you're more capable than you realize. Trust that your talents are needed, and allow yourself to step into visibility with confidence.

Affirmation & Gratitude

I take purposeful steps toward my dreams, aligning ambition with truth.

Pisces
15 September 2026

Pisces, today the stars encourage introspection. You may feel pulled inward, needing time to process emotions or recent events. Solitude is not avoidance—it's self-care. Spiritual practices feel especially potent now; meditation or journaling may bring insights that shift your perspective. Protect your energy, and don't be afraid to say no to external demands. By honoring your inner world, you create strength to face the outer one.

Affirmation & Gratitude

I embrace solitude as a sacred act of renewal and clarity.

Pisces
16 September 2026

Pisces, today's Full Moon in Pisces illuminates your identity and personal path. Emotions may feel heightened, but they are guiding you toward self-awareness. This lunation highlights who you are becoming, encouraging you to release roles, fears, or masks that no longer serve you. Allow yourself to step into authenticity without apology. This is a powerful moment of rebirth, where your spirit feels renewed. Celebrate yourself and trust your light to shine.

Affirmation & Gratitude

I embrace my authentic self, celebrating the light I bring to the world.

Pisces
17 September 2026

Pisces, the day after your Full Moon may feel emotionally tender. You've shed a layer of yourself, and now comes integration. Don't push for quick answers or action—allow yourself time to rest, reflect, and settle into this new sense of identity. Conversations with trusted friends or journaling can help anchor the lessons revealed. The cosmos reminds you that growth is a process, not an instant leap. Gentle self-compassion is your greatest ally today.

Affirmation & Gratitude

I give myself grace as I integrate change, trusting growth unfolds in its own time.

Pisces
18 September 2026

Pisces, today the energy shifts toward your resources and values. You may feel nudged to examine how you manage your finances, time, and energy. Ask yourself whether these reflect what truly matters to you. If misalignment appears, small adjustments can restore balance. The universe reminds you that security grows when it's built on authenticity. Prosperity is not only material —it also includes emotional and spiritual richness. Align all three for lasting stability.

Affirmation & Gratitude

I align my resources with my values, creating true abundance in all areas of life.

Pisces
19 September 2026

Pisces, curiosity is strong today. You may feel inspired to learn, explore, or expand your horizons through study, travel, or deep conversation. Even the smallest shift in routine can open you to new wisdom. Pay attention to synchronicities—they may guide you to the right book, mentor, or opportunity. Your spirit thrives when it's open to growth. Don't be afraid to take a step into the unfamiliar; it could be exactly what you need.

Affirmation & Gratitude

I welcome new learning, trusting curiosity to guide my growth.

Pisces
20 September 2026

Pisces, career and recognition come into focus. Your talents may be noticed by others, or you may feel motivated to step more fully into your purpose. Practical action will yield results today—don't underestimate the power of small, consistent effort. Ask yourself whether your ambitions align with your truth. The universe supports progress, but only if it reflects authenticity. Trust your path and step forward with quiet confidence.

Affirmation & Gratitude

I take purposeful steps toward my true calling, aligning ambition with authenticity.

Pisces
21 September 2026

Pisces, today invites rest and inner reflection. Your sensitivity may feel heightened, making solitude especially nourishing. Don't mistake stillness for stagnation—it's preparing you for what comes next. Dreams or intuitive whispers may feel vivid and carry important messages. Allow yourself to retreat, knowing you're recharging your energy. This pause is necessary, and it will restore clarity and balance.

Affirmation & Gratitude

I embrace rest as sacred, trusting reflection renews my spirit.

Pisces
22 September 2026

Pisces, transformation energy rises strongly today. You may feel emotions surfacing, pointing you to what you're ready to release. Whether it's an outdated belief, a lingering fear, or a draining situation, the cosmos is asking you to let it go. This isn't about loss —it's about creating freedom. Embrace change with courage; it's moving you closer to your authentic self. Transformation today may feel powerful and deeply cleansing.

Affirmation & Gratitude

I release what no longer serves, welcoming transformation with trust.

Pisces
23 September 2026

Pisces, the Sun shifts into Libra today, activating your sector of shared resources, intimacy, and transformation. Over the coming weeks, themes around finances, trust, and vulnerability will come into focus. Today may already highlight where balance is needed in your closest connections—whether financial, emotional, or energetic. Don't shy away from honest conversations; they can bring clarity and healing. This is also a time for deep personal growth. You are being guided to release what keeps you from true intimacy and empowerment.

Affirmation & Gratitude

I embrace honesty and balance, welcoming transformation in my closest connections.

Pisces
24 September 2026

Pisces, today emphasizes daily routines and wellbeing. You may feel a push to tidy up your schedule, bring order to chaos, or tend to your body's needs. Even small changes, like adjusting sleep patterns or organizing your time, can bring long-term harmony. The stars remind you that your daily habits shape your future—choose those that honor your energy. Consistency is more important than perfection, so take it step by step.

Affirmation & Gratitude

I create supportive habits that nurture my body, mind, and spirit.

Pisces
25 September 2026

Pisces, today's cosmic energy highlights relationships. You may feel more aware of the dynamics in your partnerships, noticing where harmony flows and where adjustments are needed. This is a great day for open-hearted conversations, especially if something has been left unsaid. Balance is key—remember to honor your needs while respecting others. Love and connection grow stronger when honesty and care flow both ways.

Affirmation & Gratitude

I welcome harmony in my relationships, honoring balance and mutual respect.

Pisces
26 September 2026

Pisces, today invites you to focus on self-care and health. You may feel inspired to refine routines or make decisions that support long-term wellness. Pay attention to your body's signals—they're guiding you toward balance. This isn't about restriction but about nurturing yourself with kindness. Small adjustments today create ripple effects that benefit you later. Approach change gently and consistently, and your energy will grow stronger each day.

Affirmation & Gratitude

I nurture my body with kindness, creating harmony through daily choices.

Pisces
27 September 2026

Pisces, today's energy emphasizes exploration and growth. You may feel inspired to learn something new, engage in stimulating conversations, or broaden your worldview. The universe is reminding you that wisdom often comes from stepping outside your comfort zone. Say yes to opportunities that excite your spirit—even small adventures can spark lasting inspiration. Stay open to signs and synchronicities, as they will point you toward valuable lessons.

Affirmation & Gratitude

I embrace curiosity as my guide, welcoming growth through new experiences.

Pisces
28 September 2026

Pisces, career and long-term purpose are highlighted today. You may receive recognition for your contributions or feel a surge of clarity about your next professional step. Don't ignore inner nudges—they're pointing you toward alignment. Even small actions, like refining plans or reaching out to a mentor, can shift momentum. Trust that progress doesn't always have to be grand; consistent effort matters most. Align ambition with authenticity for true fulfillment.

Affirmation & Gratitude

I step into purpose with confidence, trusting my path unfolds with meaning.

Pisces
29 September 2026

Pisces, today encourages rest and inner reflection. You may feel sensitive or introspective, and solitude will help you recharge. Dreams may carry important guidance, so pay close attention to symbols or feelings that arise. This is a good day to slow down, meditate, or spend time in nature. By honoring your need for quiet, you'll emerge with renewed clarity and energy for the days ahead.

Affirmation & Gratitude

I honor stillness, trusting it restores balance and clarity within me.

Pisces
30 September 2026

Pisces, today transformation energy feels especially strong. You may notice old fears, attachments, or patterns resurfacing—not to hold you back, but to show you what is ready to be released. This is a day of deep emotional honesty. The universe is asking you to let go of what no longer supports your growth. Though it may feel uncomfortable, liberation awaits on the other side of surrender. Trust that shedding the old is making space for something truer to your spirit.

Affirmation & Gratitude

I release with courage, trusting transformation clears space for renewal.

October 2026

Pisces
01 October 2026

Pisces, a new month begins with energy focused on friendships and community. You may feel called to connect with like-minded people or invest in a group effort that inspires you. Pay attention to which relationships fuel you with joy and which ones leave you drained. The stars remind you that authentic community strengthens your spirit, while shallow ties weigh you down. Celebrate the connections that uplift you and honor your individuality.

Affirmation & Gratitude

I welcome friendships that inspire me and align with my authentic self.

Pisces
02 October 2026

Pisces, today's energy encourages quiet reflection and solitude. You may crave time away from the noise of life, seeking peace in your inner world. This is a powerful day for journaling, meditation, or dream work. Insights may arrive in subtle ways, helping you understand where you're headed next. Don't feel guilty for slowing down—your spirit needs this pause to restore balance and clarity.

Affirmation & Gratitude

I honor solitude as sacred, allowing wisdom to rise in stillness.

Pisces
03 October 2026

Pisces, curiosity and exploration are highlighted today. You may feel drawn toward learning, travel, or engaging with new philosophies. Conversations could spark inspiration, or synchronicities may guide you toward something that shifts your perspective. The cosmos is encouraging you to step beyond what feels familiar. Even a small step into new territory will open doors of growth and insight. Trust that curiosity is pointing you exactly where you need to go.

Affirmation & Gratitude

I embrace curiosity, trusting it leads me to wisdom and growth.

Pisces
04 October 2026

Pisces, today career and recognition take the spotlight. You may feel a surge of motivation to focus on your goals, or perhaps you'll receive acknowledgment for past efforts. Align your ambitions with your heart, not external pressure. Practical planning will move you forward now. A conversation with a mentor or leader could bring valuable guidance. Trust that the path ahead becomes clearer when you act with integrity and confidence.

Affirmation & Gratitude

I align ambition with authenticity, stepping toward success with confidence.

Pisces
05 October 2026

Pisces, today's cosmic energy encourages rest and self-care. Your sensitivity may feel heightened, and solitude will help you restore balance. Avoid overextending yourself; instead, spend time doing what soothes your spirit. Dreams or intuitive nudges may carry meaningful messages. This isn't a day for pushing forward—it's a day for renewal. Honor your inner rhythm, and trust that clarity will follow once you've taken time to recharge.

Affirmation & Gratitude

I restore my energy through rest, trusting renewal is part of progress.

Pisces
06 October 2026

Pisces, transformation is in focus again today. Emotional intensity may surface, showing you where you've outgrown certain patterns or attachments. This is the universe's way of helping you evolve. Though uncomfortable at times, these shifts create freedom and authenticity. Release with love and gratitude—what leaves now is making room for something that truly aligns with your higher path. Transformation is not an ending but the beginning of a new chapter.

Affirmation & Gratitude

I release with love, opening my heart to transformation and growth.

Pisces
07 October 2026

Pisces, friendships and community connections are highlighted today. You may feel inspired to reach out to friends, collaborate, or join a group that aligns with your values. Notice how your energy feels in certain circles—if it uplifts you, lean in; if it drains you, consider pulling back. Collective energy can bring inspiration and joy, but only when it reflects authenticity. The universe is reminding you to align socially with what feels true to your spirit.

Affirmation & Gratitude

I connect with communities that uplift me and reflect my authentic self.

Pisces
08 October 2026

Pisces, today calls for quiet reflection and spiritual awareness. You may crave solitude or feel guided toward practices that restore your inner balance. Journaling, meditation, or even mindful silence will be powerful tools for clarity. Dreams may carry guidance, so pay attention to details and symbols. This is not a day for rushing forward but for tuning into your soul's whispers. Rest is renewal, not wasted time.

Affirmation & Gratitude

I honor solitude, trusting stillness brings me clarity and strength.

Pisces
09 October 2026

Pisces, the stars encourage expansion today. You may feel curious, eager to learn, or drawn toward conversations that broaden your perspective. A chance encounter, inspiring book, or travel opportunity could spark a shift in outlook. The cosmos invites you to stay open and let curiosity guide you. Growth doesn't always happen in leaps—it often begins with a small spark of inspiration that changes everything.

Affirmation & Gratitude

I welcome new experiences, trusting curiosity to guide me toward growth.

Pisces
10 October 2026

Pisces, career matters may come into focus. Recognition could arrive for your efforts, or you may feel motivated to set clearer goals for your future. Don't ignore inner nudges if they suggest you're ready for change. Align ambition with authenticity—when your work reflects your values, success feels fulfilling, not hollow. Take one concrete step today toward your bigger vision. Even small actions will carry long-term impact.

Affirmation & Gratitude

I align my goals with my truth, taking steps toward meaningful success.

Pisces
11 October 2026

Pisces, today emphasizes rest and reflection. Your heightened sensitivity may make you want to step back from busyness and honor your inner rhythm. Listen to your body and spirit—if they crave stillness, give it freely. Intuitive insights may surface in dreams or quiet moments. Avoid rushing decisions; wisdom will emerge in its own timing. This is a day to care for yourself and recharge without guilt.

Affirmation & Gratitude

I give myself permission to rest, knowing renewal is essential.

Pisces
12 October 2026

Pisces, today transformation may feel strong again. Emotions could rise, pointing to habits, beliefs, or attachments you've outgrown. Though the process can feel challenging, it is deeply healing. By releasing what no longer serves, you create freedom for what is aligned to enter. Remember, transformation is a gift, not a loss—it clears your path of weight and brings renewal. Trust that what's unfolding is guiding you toward authenticity.

Affirmation & Gratitude

I release the old with love, embracing transformation as my ally.

Pisces
13 October 2026

Pisces, today the cosmos highlights friendships and social bonds. Conversations may feel more meaningful, and group connections could spark fresh ideas. Pay attention to who inspires you and who doesn't—your energy deserves to be honored. Collaboration is favored, but only in circles where you feel celebrated, not drained. Choose wisely where you share your time. True community uplifts, encourages, and reflects your growth.

Affirmation & Gratitude

I welcome friendships that inspire and uplift me, honoring authentic community.

Pisces
14 October 2026

Pisces, today the cosmos invites you to pause and look inward. You may feel more sensitive, craving time away from noise and external demands. This is a day for meditation, journaling, or dreamwork, as your subconscious is rich with insights now. Don't pressure yourself to have everything figured out—the answers are forming in stillness. Allow yourself to rest without guilt, trusting that the wisdom you seek will surface in divine timing.

Affirmation & Gratitude

I honor quiet reflection, knowing stillness reveals truth and clarity.

Pisces
15 October 2026

Pisces, transformation energy rises again. Old emotions or patterns may resurface, giving you the opportunity to finally let them go. Though the process may stir intensity, trust that it is clearing space for growth. A conversation or realization could illuminate what needs release. Embrace change with courage, knowing it is aligning you more deeply with your authentic self. This is a powerful day to shed the old and welcome the new.

Affirmation & Gratitude

I release the past with courage, opening space for renewal and freedom.

Pisces
16 October 2026

Pisces, today friendships and networks take the spotlight. You may feel called to connect with like-minded people who share your vision, or you may realize certain connections no longer align. Collaboration can be fruitful, but only if everyone brings respect and authenticity to the table. The cosmos encourages you to invest in communities that uplift and inspire you. Choose carefully where you place your energy.

Affirmation & Gratitude

I cherish uplifting friendships that celebrate authenticity and growth.

Pisces
17 October 2026

Pisces, today's energy draws you inward again. Solitude may feel appealing as your spirit seeks space to process emotions or recent experiences. Pay close attention to intuitive nudges—they may hold guidance for decisions you've been considering. Don't feel pressured to socialize or be overly productive. The universe reminds you that rest is part of progress. Gentle self-care will leave you renewed and aligned.

Affirmation & Gratitude

I embrace solitude as healing, trusting inner wisdom to guide me.

Pisces
18 October 2026

Pisces, curiosity and expansion are emphasized today. You may feel drawn to learning, exploring, or engaging in conversations that broaden your understanding of the world. Travel, even short distances, could also be meaningful. Allow yourself to explore beyond your comfort zone—the universe is nudging you toward new horizons. Growth thrives when you say yes to discovery, no matter how small the step.

Affirmation & Gratitude

I welcome growth through exploration, trusting curiosity to guide me forward.

Pisces
19 October 2026

Pisces, career and long-term goals come into focus. Recognition for your dedication may arrive, or you may feel called to refine your ambitions. Aligning your goals with your heart ensures that success feels fulfilling, not empty. Even small steps today—sending a message, updating your vision, or completing a task—can create lasting momentum. Trust that steady progress builds toward meaningful achievement.

Affirmation & Gratitude

I align ambition with authenticity, taking steps that honor my true path.

Pisces
20 October 2026

Pisces, today's energy emphasizes rest and restoration. Your sensitivity may feel heightened, so take time to retreat and recharge. This is a day for self-care rituals—long baths, meditation, or simply enjoying quiet. Don't push for productivity; instead, allow yourself to replenish. Dreams or subtle signs may bring insights if you create space for them to surface. The cosmos reminds you that renewal fuels future growth.

Affirmation & Gratitude

I nurture myself through rest, trusting renewal strengthens my spirit.

Pisces
21 October 2026

Pisces, today transformation energy is strong. You may find yourself facing truths you've avoided, whether about relationships, habits, or personal fears. While it might feel uncomfortable, this is the universe's way of clearing your path. Release with compassion, not judgment. Remember, endings are not losses—they are openings. What leaves now is making space for growth. Trust that you're being reshaped into alignment with your authentic self. Transformation is your ally, guiding you into renewal.

Affirmation & Gratitude

I release with love and courage, embracing transformation as a step toward freedom.

Pisces
22 October 2026

Pisces, friendships and social connections are highlighted today. You may feel uplifted by the presence of like-minded people, or perhaps collaboration brings inspiration. Pay attention to which relationships energize you and which ones deplete you. The cosmos encourages you to focus on authentic community—connections built on respect, inspiration, and mutual support. Surround yourself with those who see and celebrate your true self.

Affirmation & Gratitude

I align with friendships that uplift me and reflect my authenticity.

Pisces
23 October 2026

Pisces, the Sun moves into Scorpio today, illuminating your sector of exploration, higher learning, and spirituality. Over the next few weeks, you'll feel called to expand your horizons—through study, travel, or deep conversations. Today marks the beginning of this shift, urging you to seek experiences that broaden your worldview. The universe is reminding you that curiosity leads to growth and that wisdom is waiting in unexpected places.

Affirmation & Gratitude

I embrace exploration, trusting curiosity to guide me toward wisdom.

Pisces
24 October 2026

Pisces, today the cosmos turns your focus toward career and purpose. You may feel a burst of clarity about your ambitions or receive recognition for your dedication. Aligning your goals with your truth ensures your success feels fulfilling, not hollow. Take practical action today, even a small step—it will set momentum in motion. The stars remind you that persistence combined with authenticity builds lasting achievement.

Affirmation & Gratitude

I take purposeful steps toward success, aligning ambition with authenticity.

Pisces
25 October 2026

Pisces, today emphasizes rest and reflection. Your energy may feel quieter, and your spirit may crave stillness. Don't ignore this call—solitude is restorative, not isolating. Dreams may be especially vivid, offering insights into situations you've been navigating. Pay attention to subtle signs—they are guiding you. Allow yourself to retreat and recharge, trusting that clarity will surface when you honor your inner rhythm.

Affirmation & Gratitude

I embrace rest as renewal, trusting stillness restores my clarity.

Pisces
26 October 2026

Pisces, transformation energy stirs again. Old beliefs, attachments, or patterns may rise to the surface, showing you what needs release. Though the process may be emotional, it's also liberating. By shedding what no longer serves you, you open the door to growth. Today may bring a powerful realization that helps you step into greater freedom. Trust that change is leading you toward your most authentic self.

Affirmation & Gratitude

I let go with courage, knowing transformation brings freedom and alignment.

Pisces
27 October 2026

Pisces, today highlights friendships and community bonds. Group connections may feel particularly meaningful, sparking joy and collaboration. At the same time, you may recognize where boundaries are needed to protect your energy. Authentic friendships will energize you, while shallow ones may feel draining. The stars encourage you to celebrate the people who uplift you and gracefully release those who don't.

Affirmation & Gratitude

I cherish authentic friendships that bring joy and inspiration to my life.

Pisces
28 October 2026

Pisces, today's energy turns you inward. You may crave solitude, sensing that your spirit needs time to rest and reset. This is an excellent day for journaling, meditation, or simply being in nature. Dreams may be vivid, offering glimpses of guidance for your future. Avoid pushing yourself into productivity; renewal comes through stillness now. Trust that this pause is preparing you for the clarity and strength needed in the days ahead.

Affirmation & Gratitude

I honor rest as sacred, allowing solitude to restore my clarity and balance.

Pisces
29 October 2026

Pisces, transformation energy rises again, encouraging you to release outdated beliefs, fears, or attachments. While it may feel uncomfortable, trust that these endings are guiding you toward freedom and growth. A conversation or realization could help you see what's ready to shift. The cosmos reminds you that every release creates space for renewal. Embrace change with courage —it's shaping you into alignment with your truest self.

Affirmation & Gratitude

I release with trust, knowing transformation creates space for authentic growth.

Pisces
30 October 2026

Pisces, friendships and community connections are highlighted today. You may feel drawn to spend time with people who uplift and inspire you, or you could find yourself reevaluating which circles truly support your spirit. Collaboration may spark creativity and joy, but ensure you're giving your energy to those who respect your authenticity. Celebrate the connections that bring you light while gently stepping back from those that no longer resonate.

Affirmation & Gratitude

I value friendships that inspire joy and honor my true self.

Pisces
31 October 2026

Pisces, today's cosmic energy invites reflection and spiritual awareness. On this day of endings and veils thinning, your intuition feels especially sharp. Pay attention to dreams, symbols, or subtle nudges—they may reveal hidden truths. Solitude and ritual will be especially powerful, helping you connect with your inner world or spiritual practices. Avoid overextending socially; instead, honor your need for introspection and inner connection.

Affirmation & Gratitude

I trust my intuition and embrace the wisdom revealed in stillness.

November 2026

Pisces
01 November 2026

Pisces, the new month begins with curiosity and expansion. You may feel drawn toward study, travel, or experiences that broaden your perspective. Inspiration could come from a book, a mentor, or even a chance encounter. The universe is encouraging you to remain open to new ideas—your spirit thrives when learning and discovery are present. Growth doesn't have to be dramatic; even small shifts can spark lasting change.

Affirmation & Gratitude

I welcome new experiences with openness, trusting growth flows from curiosity.

Pisces
02 November 2026

Pisces, career and long-term ambitions are in the spotlight today. Recognition may arrive for your efforts, or you may feel motivated to take bold steps toward your goals. Align your ambitions with your values to ensure fulfillment. Don't ignore inner nudges that suggest it's time to pivot or refine your plans. Practical action taken today, even small, will ripple into meaningful progress in the weeks ahead.

Affirmation & Gratitude

I align my goals with my truth, taking steps toward meaningful success.

Pisces

03 November 2026

Pisces, today's energy encourages rest and inner renewal. You may feel sensitive, and solitude will help you restore balance. Dreams may be particularly vivid and worth reflecting on, as they may reveal guidance for your path ahead. This is not a day for rushing or overcommitting. Instead, honor your need for quiet, gentle care. The universe reminds you that self-restoration is a vital part of progress.

Affirmation & Gratitude

I embrace rest as renewal, trusting stillness restores my strength and wisdom.

Pisces
04 November 2026

Pisces, transformation themes continue today. You may feel prompted to release a long-held habit, attachment, or even a limiting belief. This process may stir emotions, but it is clearing your path for freedom. Trust that what feels heavy now is lightening your load for the future. A conversation or reflection may act as a catalyst for this shift. Remember, change is not a loss—it's the space where new beginnings emerge.

Affirmation & Gratitude

I let go with love, trusting transformation to lead me into greater freedom.

Pisces
05 November 2026

Pisces, today shines a light on friendships and community bonds. Group activities may be uplifting, or you may discover who truly values your energy. Collaboration feels powerful, but only when it's mutual and authentic. The cosmos is reminding you that your spirit thrives in environments where respect and inspiration are present. Celebrate those who align with you, and don't be afraid to distance yourself from draining connections.

Affirmation & Gratitude

I align with authentic friendships that uplift and celebrate my spirit.

Pisces
06 November 2026

Pisces, today's energy turns inward. You may crave solitude, feeling more sensitive to the outside world than usual. This is a day for spiritual practices, meditation, or rest. Pay attention to your dreams or intuitive nudges—they carry guidance for your path. Stillness is not wasted—it is renewal. Allow yourself to withdraw without guilt, trusting that your energy will be replenished by quiet reflection.

Affirmation & Gratitude

I embrace solitude as sacred, trusting it restores clarity and peace.

Pisces
07 November 2026

Pisces, curiosity and learning are emphasized today. You may feel called to explore a new subject, engage in stimulating conversation, or seek out inspiration through books or media. Even small moments of openness can spark big shifts in understanding. Travel, even short, may also be meaningful now. The universe is asking you to say yes to experiences that expand your worldview. Growth thrives when curiosity leads the way.

Affirmation & Gratitude

I welcome growth through curiosity, allowing wisdom to flow into my life.

Pisces
08 November 2026

Pisces, career and long-term goals come to the forefront today. Recognition for your past efforts could arrive, or you may feel inspired to pursue your ambitions more clearly. Align your professional path with your values and passions—when authenticity leads, fulfillment follows. Take practical steps today, no matter how small, to reinforce your vision. The cosmos supports ambition when it's rooted in truth and integrity.

Affirmation & Gratitude

I take steps toward my goals, aligning ambition with my authentic self.

Pisces
09 November 2026

Pisces, today invites rest and spiritual connection. You may feel more attuned to subtle energies and require quiet space to integrate them. Don't push yourself into busyness—your inner world needs attention. Journaling, meditation, or time in nature will help you recharge. Intuitive insights may arrive, so keep an open heart to receive them. Stillness today is fuel for the momentum you'll need soon.

Affirmation & Gratitude

I honor rest as renewal, trusting stillness to restore my spirit.

Pisces
10 November 2026

Pisces, transformation rises again today. The universe may highlight areas of your life that feel outdated, showing you what is ready to leave. Release doesn't always mean drastic change—it can be as simple as shifting a perspective or letting go of self-doubt. Trust that endings make way for beginnings. This process is aligning you with authenticity and freedom. Though it may feel emotional, liberation lies in surrender.

Affirmation & Gratitude

I release with courage, trusting transformation to lead me into alignment.

Pisces
11 November 2026

Pisces, today shines a light on friendships and your broader community. You may feel inspired to connect with like-minded people who share your passions and dreams. Collaborations can flourish now, sparking creativity and joy. Pay close attention to which groups energize you and which drain your spirit—the difference will be obvious today. The cosmos asks you to invest only in connections that reflect respect and authenticity. This ensures your energy is used in uplifting ways.

Affirmation & Gratitude

I cherish communities that celebrate authenticity and inspire my spirit to grow.

Pisces
12 November 2026

Pisces, today invites you into quiet reflection. You may feel more sensitive, picking up on subtle energies from those around you. Solitude will restore your balance. This is an ideal time for meditation, journaling, or connecting with your intuition. Dreams may be particularly vivid, offering guidance for your next steps. Don't see rest as wasted—it's an essential part of your cycle of growth and clarity.

Affirmation & Gratitude

I embrace solitude as sacred, trusting it restores clarity and peace within me.

Pisces
13 November 2026

Pisces, curiosity is alive today. You may be drawn toward new ideas, philosophies, or experiences that expand your perspective. Conversations could bring surprising insights, or you may feel pulled to study or travel. The stars encourage you to follow your curiosity, even if it feels unfamiliar. Growth often begins with a single step into the unknown. Allow yourself to explore—the universe is guiding you toward wisdom and inspiration.

Affirmation & Gratitude

I welcome new perspectives, trusting curiosity to lead me to growth.

Pisces
14 November 2026

Pisces, career and purpose take center stage. You may feel motivated to set clearer goals or take practical steps toward your ambitions. Recognition for your hard work may arrive, or a mentor could offer guidance that sparks direction. The cosmos reminds you to align ambition with authenticity—success feels sweeter when it reflects your soul. Even small, deliberate actions today can ripple into long-term achievement.

Affirmation & Gratitude

I align my goals with my truth, taking steady steps toward meaningful success.

Pisces
15 November 2026

Pisces, today emphasizes rest and introspection. Your spirit may feel sensitive, needing quiet to process recent shifts. Spiritual practices like meditation, journaling, or simply sitting in silence will bring peace and guidance. Avoid overcommitting—your energy is best spent on self-care. Dreams may be especially vivid, carrying messages worth noting. This is not a day for pushing outward but for nourishing your inner world.

Affirmation & Gratitude

I honor rest and reflection, knowing they restore my balance and wisdom.

Pisces
16 November 2026

Pisces, today transformation energy rises once more. You may feel emotions stirring, pointing you toward what you've outgrown. Whether it's an outdated habit, a draining relationship, or a limiting belief, the universe is urging you to release it. Though uncomfortable, this process frees you for new beginnings. Lean into self-compassion —change is easier when you support yourself with kindness. Remember, transformation is not loss, but liberation.

Affirmation & Gratitude

I release with love, trusting transformation aligns me with my authentic path.

Pisces
17 November 2026

Pisces, friendships and collaborations are emphasized today. You may feel inspired to connect with groups or communities that align with your dreams. Teamwork may bring progress, and uplifting conversations could fuel your motivation. Notice where your energy feels celebrated and where it feels dismissed—choose wisely where to invest yourself. True community brings joy, creativity, and encouragement. Celebrate the people who inspire and uplift you.

Affirmation & Gratitude

I value friendships that inspire growth and celebrate my authenticity.

Pisces
18 November 2026

Pisces, today your energy turns inward. You may feel more sensitive than usual, picking up on the emotions of others easily. Protect your energy and focus on your own inner balance. This is a day to recharge through meditation, journaling, or simply enjoying solitude. Dreams may hold meaning, so pay attention to symbols and emotions that surface. Don't see this retreat as withdrawal—it's self-care, and it allows you to return to the world renewed.

Affirmation & Gratitude

I honor solitude as sacred, letting stillness restore my clarity and peace.

Pisces
19 November 2026

Pisces, transformation is in focus today. Old patterns, habits, or fears may resurface, showing you what still needs to be released. Though the process may stir deep emotions, it's guiding you toward freedom and authenticity. The universe asks you to trust the journey of letting go. Release doesn't mean loss—it means clearing the way for something more aligned. This is a powerful day for breakthroughs and emotional healing.

Affirmation & Gratitude

I release with courage, trusting transformation brings me freedom and renewal.

Pisces
20 November 2026

Pisces, today shines a light on friendships and community. You may feel drawn to connect with like-minded people or collaborate on shared goals. Notice which groups truly support and inspire you, and which drain your energy. Authenticity is key —invest your time where you feel valued and respected. Shared purpose can bring joy and inspiration, while shallow ties only hold you back. Choose wisely and celebrate genuine connection.

Affirmation & Gratitude

I cherish friendships that uplift and align with my true self.

Pisces
21 November 2026

Pisces, today's energy draws you toward reflection and spiritual awareness. You may crave quiet time, away from busyness, to listen to your inner voice. This is a powerful day for rituals, meditation, or creative flow that connects you with your intuition. Don't pressure yourself to act; clarity will arise naturally from stillness. Trust the signs and synchronicities—they're pointing you toward your next step.

Affirmation & Gratitude

I embrace stillness, trusting my intuition to reveal the path ahead.

Pisces
22 November 2026

Pisces, the Sun moves into Sagittarius today, highlighting your career and life purpose for the weeks ahead. You'll feel called to focus on ambitions, long-term goals, and the ways you want to share your gifts with the world. Today may already bring clarity or recognition, reminding you of your strengths. Align ambition with truth, not external pressure. Success feels fulfilling when it reflects who you truly are.

Affirmation & Gratitude

I align my ambitions with authenticity, stepping into purpose with confidence.

Pisces
23 November 2026

Pisces, today emphasizes rest and renewal. You may feel more sensitive to external pressures, making solitude especially healing. Allow yourself to step back from obligations if possible. Dreams may be vivid and worth recording, as they may carry guidance. The cosmos reminds you that taking care of yourself is not selfish—it's essential. Stillness will prepare you for the productivity and clarity coming soon.

Affirmation & Gratitude

I nurture myself with rest, trusting renewal strengthens my spirit.

Pisces
24 November 2026

Pisces, today transformation energy feels powerful. Emotional truths may surface, helping you see clearly what you've outgrown. Release may not come easily, but the freedom it creates is undeniable. Whether in relationships, habits, or old beliefs, trust that letting go aligns you with your higher path. Transformation today may feel like a breakthrough—allow yourself to move forward with courage and compassion.

Affirmation & Gratitude

I release the old with love, welcoming transformation as freedom.

Pisces
25 November 2026

Pisces, today emphasizes friendships and social connections. You may feel drawn to collaborate or spend time with people who share your passions. Group activities may bring joy, but they will also reveal which connections truly nourish you and which leave you drained. The stars remind you to honor your energy and choose relationships built on respect and inspiration. Celebrate authentic bonds and let go of shallow ties.

Affirmation & Gratitude

I invest in friendships that inspire joy and honor my authentic self.

Pisces
26 November 2026

Pisces, today's cosmic flow draws you inward. You may feel more reflective, noticing subtle shifts in your emotions. This is an ideal day for spiritual practices, dream journaling, or simply creating stillness. Pay attention to intuitive nudges; they're guiding you toward clarity. Avoid overcommitting—quiet moments are more important than busyness. Renewal happens when you honor your inner needs above external demands.

Affirmation & Gratitude

I honor stillness, trusting it restores clarity and balance within me.

Pisces
27 November 2026

Pisces, transformation energy continues to rise today. Something you've been holding onto may feel heavier than usual, showing you it's ready to be released. Though letting go is rarely easy, it opens the door to growth and freedom. This process may bring emotional intensity, but it also carries healing. Trust that you're evolving into a truer version of yourself. Surrender what no longer serves, and embrace the space being created.

Affirmation & Gratitude

I release with courage, welcoming transformation as a path to freedom.

Pisces
28 November 2026

Pisces, today highlights curiosity and learning. You may feel inspired to explore new ideas, cultures, or philosophies. A book, a conversation, or even a chance encounter could shift your perspective. The stars are encouraging you to embrace openness and allow your worldview to expand. Growth often begins with small steps, so don't underestimate the power of exploration. Inspiration and wisdom are waiting to meet you.

Affirmation & Gratitude

I welcome new perspectives, trusting curiosity to guide me into growth.

Pisces
29 November 2026

Pisces, career and long-term goals are highlighted today. Recognition for your dedication may arrive, or you may feel motivated to refine your vision. Ask yourself if your current direction aligns with your truth. Authentic ambition leads to meaningful success. Practical steps taken today will carry momentum. A conversation with a mentor or colleague could also provide clarity and encouragement.

Affirmation & Gratitude

I align ambition with authenticity, taking steady steps toward my purpose.

Pisces
30 November 2026

Pisces, today's energy emphasizes rest and reflection. You may feel more sensitive to external demands, so retreat where possible. Stillness is a powerful tool now—your spirit needs quiet to integrate lessons from the past month. Dreams or intuitive whispers may offer guidance if you create space to listen. Don't feel guilty for slowing down—your energy is best used for renewal today.

Affirmation & Gratitude

I embrace rest as sacred, trusting reflection restores my spirit.

December 2026

Pisces
01 December 2026

Pisces, the new month begins with transformative energy. You may feel emotions surfacing, pointing to what you've outgrown. The universe is urging you to release habits, fears, or attachments that weigh you down. Though the process may feel intense, it clears your path for authentic growth. Transformation is not about loss—it's about freedom. Trust that you're stepping into a new chapter where alignment and renewal guide the way.

Affirmation & Gratitude

I release the old with gratitude, embracing transformation as my ally.

Pisces
02 December 2026

Pisces, today highlights friendships and community. You may feel drawn to spend time with like-minded souls or collaborate on a project that excites you. Group energy can be uplifting now, but notice how your spirit feels—authentic connections energize, while shallow ones may leave you drained. Invest in bonds that encourage growth and reflect mutual respect. The cosmos reminds you that your circle shapes your spirit, so choose wisely.

Affirmation & Gratitude

I surround myself with friendships that uplift and inspire my spirit.

Pisces
03 December 2026

Pisces, your inner world calls for attention today. Sensitivity may feel heightened, making solitude more appealing. Dreams or intuitive nudges may bring guidance, especially if you create quiet space to listen. Don't pressure yourself to achieve outwardly; inner renewal is your focus. A spiritual practice, even a simple one, will help you feel grounded. Stillness now will prepare you for clearer action in the days ahead.

Affirmation & Gratitude

I honor solitude and reflection, trusting stillness to renew my clarity.

Pisces
04 December 2026

Pisces, transformation themes rise again. You may be prompted to release something you've been clinging to, whether it's an outdated belief, fear, or dynamic. Though it may feel emotional, letting go will liberate you. The universe is guiding you toward alignment with your higher self. Today may also bring a powerful realization about what's holding you back and how to free yourself. Trust the process—it's preparing you for growth.

Affirmation & Gratitude

I release with love, knowing transformation clears space for new beginnings.

Pisces
05 December 2026

Pisces, curiosity and exploration are emphasized. You may feel inspired to learn, travel, or engage with new perspectives that broaden your worldview. Conversations could spark insights, or a chance encounter may shift your direction. Say yes to opportunities that expand your vision, even in small ways. Growth often begins with openness to the unknown. Trust that curiosity is leading you toward inspiration and wisdom.

Affirmation & Gratitude

I embrace curiosity, welcoming growth through new perspectives.

Pisces
06 December 2026

Pisces, your career and ambitions may come into sharper focus today. Recognition could arrive, or you may feel motivated to refine your goals. The stars encourage you to align your professional path with authenticity—when your work reflects your truth, fulfillment follows naturally. Practical steps today, however small, carry weight and move you closer to long-term success. Don't underestimate the power of consistency.

Affirmation & Gratitude

I take purposeful steps toward success, aligning ambition with authenticity.

Pisces
07 December 2026

Pisces, today's energy turns inward. You may feel more attuned to your spiritual side, sensing the need for rest and reflection. Intuitive insights may surface in dreams or quiet moments—don't dismiss them. This is a powerful day for inner work and self-care. Avoid external distractions where possible; instead, nourish your spirit with stillness and gentleness. Renewal is happening beneath the surface, preparing you for growth.

Affirmation & Gratitude

I honor rest as sacred, trusting inner renewal to guide my next steps.

Pisces
08 December 2026

Pisces, today transformation feels intense yet purposeful. Old emotions or attachments may rise to the surface, showing you what is ready for release. While the process may feel challenging, it opens the path for greater freedom. Trust that the universe is helping you evolve into alignment with your authentic self. Release doesn't mean loss—it's an act of empowerment. Let go with love, and welcome the new energy waiting to enter.

Affirmation & Gratitude

I release the old with courage, embracing transformation as liberation.

Pisces
09 December 2026

Pisces, today highlights friendships and community. You may feel uplifted by being around people who share your passions or values. Collaboration could spark inspiration, or a group effort may move forward now. Be mindful of your energy—invest in connections that energize you and step away from those that deplete you. The stars remind you that your spirit thrives in circles of authenticity and mutual respect. Celebrate the joy of belonging while honoring your individuality.

Affirmation & Gratitude

I invest in friendships that nourish and uplift my authentic spirit.

Pisces
10 December 2026

Pisces, today invites introspection. You may feel more sensitive than usual, sensing the subtle undercurrents around you. Solitude will help you find balance. Dreams may be vivid, carrying messages for your path. Don't pressure yourself to act or achieve—your spirit needs time to process and restore. Spiritual practices like meditation or journaling will be especially powerful. By honoring quiet today, you prepare yourself for clarity tomorrow.

Affirmation & Gratitude

I honor stillness and reflection, trusting quiet moments to restore my clarity.

Pisces
11 December 2026

Pisces, transformation themes are strong today. Old emotions, fears, or patterns could resurface, reminding you of what you're ready to let go. Though the process may feel emotional, it is also empowering. Release is not loss—it's freedom. Trust the universe is guiding you to shed what no longer serves. Every step you take in letting go creates space for renewal, authenticity, and growth. Today is about courage and self-compassion in the face of change.

Affirmation & Gratitude

I release with love, welcoming transformation as my ally in growth.

Pisces
12 December 2026

Pisces, today emphasizes curiosity and exploration. You may feel inspired to learn something new, connect with a mentor, or seek experiences that broaden your perspective. Conversations may bring unexpected insights, or a small adventure could shift your outlook. The universe is asking you to stay open to new ways of thinking. Even small steps outside your comfort zone can spark lasting growth. Say yes to inspiration today.

Affirmation & Gratitude

I welcome curiosity as my guide, embracing growth in all its forms.

Pisces
13 December 2026

Pisces, today career and purpose take the spotlight. Recognition may arrive, or you may feel a surge of clarity about your long-term goals. Align your ambitions with your authentic self—true success comes when you pursue what reflects your heart. Practical steps will carry momentum now, so don't underestimate the power of small, steady actions. The stars support progress when it's rooted in integrity and truth.

Affirmation & Gratitude

I align my goals with authenticity, taking steps that honor my soul's truth.

Pisces
14 December 2026

Pisces, today's energy invites rest and spiritual connection. You may feel more attuned to your intuition and benefit from slowing down. Stillness will bring clarity, and dreams or meditative practices may reveal important guidance. Don't overload your schedule—your inner world needs attention. Honor your need for peace today, and you'll find yourself stronger and clearer tomorrow. Renewal is happening beneath the surface.

Affirmation & Gratitude

I honor rest as renewal, trusting stillness restores my strength and balance.

Pisces
15 December 2026

Pisces, transformation rises again today, reminding you of the cycles of release and renewal that shape your journey. Something you've carried for too long may feel ready to leave—perhaps an outdated belief or lingering emotional weight. Trust that letting go clears the path for growth. Though it may feel bittersweet, freedom awaits on the other side. The universe is guiding you into alignment with your truest self.

Affirmation & Gratitude

I release with gratitude, trusting transformation leads me to freedom.

Pisces
16 December 2026

Pisces, today's energy highlights friendships and community ties. You may feel drawn to connect with those who inspire you or collaborate on a meaningful project. Notice which relationships uplift you and which feel draining—the difference is clear now. Authentic bonds bring joy and support, while shallow ones leave you depleted. The universe is reminding you to invest in communities that celebrate your growth and authenticity. By choosing wisely, your social circle becomes a true source of strength.

Affirmation & Gratitude

I choose friendships that inspire joy and align with my authentic self.

Pisces
17 December 2026

Pisces, introspection is favored today. You may feel more sensitive, picking up on the subtle moods and energies around you. Solitude will help you recharge and find clarity. Dreams or meditation may bring guidance, so create time for quiet reflection. Don't feel pressured to act quickly—sometimes the best progress comes from pausing and allowing insights to surface naturally. Trust that your inner wisdom knows the way forward.

Affirmation & Gratitude

I honor stillness as sacred, trusting quiet moments to reveal guidance.

Pisces
18 December 2026

Pisces, transformation energy flows strongly today. Old fears or habits may rise, asking to be acknowledged and released. Though it may feel uncomfortable, this process is essential for your growth. The stars remind you that every ending carries the seed of a new beginning. Release with compassion rather than resistance—you're stepping into greater alignment. Trust that the universe is guiding you toward a lighter, more authentic path.

Affirmation & Gratitude

I release the old with courage, embracing transformation as renewal.

Pisces
19 December 2026

Pisces, curiosity and expansion take center stage. You may feel inspired to learn, travel, or seek out fresh perspectives. A conversation, book, or unexpected event could shift how you see the world. The cosmos encourages you to embrace opportunities that broaden your horizons. Even small steps beyond your comfort zone can spark long-term growth. Trust that your curiosity is leading you to wisdom and inspiration.

Affirmation & Gratitude

I welcome new perspectives, trusting curiosity to guide my growth.

Pisces
20 December 2026

Pisces, career and recognition are highlighted today. You may receive praise for your efforts, or you may feel ready to refine your ambitions. Align your goals with authenticity to ensure long-term fulfillment. Practical planning or a conversation with a mentor could provide clarity. Remember, true success isn't about speed—it's about moving in harmony with your soul. Trust the process and step into your purpose with confidence.

Affirmation & Gratitude

I align ambition with authenticity, taking steps that honor my soul's path.

Pisces
21 December 2026

Pisces, the Solstice arrives as the Sun enters Capricorn, illuminating your friendship and community sector. Over the coming weeks, your focus will shift to groups, shared visions, and collaborations. Today you may already sense the importance of aligning with people who reflect your values. The cosmos invites you to nurture authentic bonds and release those that no longer resonate. Connection, when rooted in truth, is your guiding light now.

Affirmation & Gratitude

I celebrate authentic community, welcoming connections that reflect my true spirit.

Pisces
22 December 2026

Pisces, today's energy invites introspection and self-care. You may feel a need to step back from social or professional demands and focus on your inner world. Dreams and intuitive nudges may be especially vivid, offering clarity if you listen closely. This is a powerful day for renewal—don't feel guilty for slowing down. The stillness you create today will help guide you into the new year with strength.

Affirmation & Gratitude

I honor rest and reflection, trusting stillness restores my spirit.

Pisces
23 December 2026

Pisces, transformation energy is strong today. You may feel prompted to release what no longer serves—perhaps an outdated belief, emotional attachment, or draining responsibility. This process may feel intense, but the freedom it creates is invaluable. The stars remind you that you cannot step into the new while clinging to the old. Trust that the endings happening now are making space for beginnings that better reflect your truth.

Affirmation & Gratitude

I release the past with love, opening myself to renewal and freedom.

Pisces
24 December 2026

Pisces, today shines a light on friendships and loved ones. You may feel a strong pull toward connection, celebration, and sharing joy. It's an ideal time to appreciate the people who bring light to your life. At the same time, you may sense where distance or boundaries are needed in relationships that no longer resonate. Honor both the joy of closeness and the wisdom of discernment.

Affirmation & Gratitude

I cherish friendships that uplift me, while setting boundaries that honor my spirit.

Pisces
25 December 2026

Pisces, on this day of celebration, your energy feels deeply intuitive and compassionate. You may feel especially connected to loved ones or find yourself reflecting on the importance of family, tradition, and love. The cosmos encourages you to embrace gratitude today—for both the blessings and the lessons. Allow joy to flow freely, and don't hesitate to share your light with others. Your presence brings warmth wherever you go.

Affirmation & Gratitude

I celebrate love, gratitude, and the joy of connection today.

Pisces
26 December 2026

Pisces, today encourages reflection and rest after recent activity. Your body and mind may need a slower pace to process emotions and recharge. Dreams or intuitive nudges may feel vivid, offering guidance for the days ahead. Avoid overcommitting—your energy is best spent on gentle self-care. Solitude isn't selfish; it's nourishment. The stillness you honor today will bring clarity and renewal.

Affirmation & Gratitude

I honor rest as sacred, trusting stillness restores my balance.

Pisces
27 December 2026

Pisces, curiosity is highlighted today. You may feel drawn to explore new ideas, try a fresh activity, or engage in meaningful conversations that broaden your perspective. The universe is encouraging you to embrace growth, even in small ways. Inspiration may come from unexpected sources—follow where it leads. Openness now can spark long-term transformation and joy. Don't be afraid to step into the unknown—it holds treasures for you.

Affirmation & Gratitude

I welcome curiosity as my guide, embracing wisdom in every form.

Pisces
28 December 2026

Pisces, career and long-term goals are emphasized today. Recognition for your efforts may arrive, or you may feel inspired to refine your ambitions. Aligning your path with authenticity is key now—success feels hollow if it doesn't reflect your truth. The cosmos supports practical steps today, so focus on actions that bring you closer to your vision. Trust that consistency, not speed, builds meaningful progress.

Affirmation & Gratitude

I align my goals with truth, taking steady steps toward meaningful success.

Pisces
29 December 2026

Pisces, today emphasizes inner reflection and self-care. The year's energy may feel heavy, making solitude more appealing. Allow yourself time to rest and process all you've experienced. Spiritual practices like meditation or journaling will feel especially nourishing. Pay attention to dreams—they may carry insights as you prepare to step into a new year. Renewal is happening beneath the surface—trust the process of slowing down.

Affirmation & Gratitude

I honor solitude and reflection, trusting rest prepares me for new beginnings.

Pisces
30 December 2026

Pisces, today carries a deeply introspective tone as the year begins winding down. You may feel reflective, looking back on 2026 and noticing both the challenges you've overcome and the growth you've achieved. Allow yourself to honor the lessons and release any lingering regrets. This is a day for gratitude and gentle closure. Solitude or quiet time with loved ones will feel especially rewarding. The stars encourage you to let go of what doesn't need to follow you into the new year. You are preparing for renewal, so clear your energy with love and intention.

Affirmation & Gratitude

I honor the lessons of this year, releasing the past with gratitude and grace.

Pisces
31 December 2026

Pisces, the final day of the year invites both reflection and celebration. You may feel emotional, sensing the endings and beginnings weaving together. Take time to acknowledge how far you've come—spiritually, emotionally, and personally. Celebrate your resilience and the wisdom you've gained. The cosmos encourages you to set intentions for 2027, focusing on what you wish to grow and create. End the year in alignment with gratitude, love, and hope. Remember, you carry everything you need within you to flourish in the year ahead. Trust yourself and step into the new cycle with courage.

Affirmation & Gratitude

I step into the new year with gratitude, courage, and hope in my heart.

www.ingramcontent.com/pod-product-compliance
Lightning Source LLC
Chambersburg PA
CBHW071145070526
44584CB00019B/2671